BE FRUITFUL AND MULTIPLY

BE FRUITFUL AND MULTIPLY

*FERTILITY THERAPY
AND THE JEWISH TRADITION*

edited by

RICHARD V. GRAZI, MD

WITH AN INTRODUCTION BY
LORD IMMANUEL JAKOBOVITS

GENESIS JERUSALEM PRESS 5754/1994

© Copyright 1994 by Richard V. Grazi

All rights reserved. No part of this publication may be translated, dramatized, reproduced, stored in a retrieval system or transmitted, **in any form** or by any means, electronic, mechanical, photocopying, recording or otherwise, without prior permission in writing from the publishers. Printed in Israel. The rights of the copyright holder will be strictly enforced.

Typeset by *Dagush* International, Ma'ale Amos, Israel.

ISBN 0-9630936-4-9

Registered in Library of Congress

FIRST EDITION

10 9 8 7 6 5 4 3 2 1

Distributed by:
FELDHEIM PUBLISHERS
200 Airport Executive Park
Spring Valley, NY 10977

J. LEHMANN
Hebrew Booksellers
20 Cambridge Terrace
Gateshead
Tyne & Wear

Printed in Israel

CONTENTS

Introduction vii
Foreword ix

I. **The Religious Jewish Infertile Couple**
   Introduction 3
   The Longing for Children in a
   Traditional Jewish Family 5
   The Rabbinic and Medical Partnership 13
   Infertility: Issues From the Heart 19
   A Rabbinic Response to Infertility 39

II. **Diagnostic Evaluations**
    Introduction 51
    Male Infertility: Halakhic Issues 55
    Diagnostic Procedures in the Female Patient 79

III. **Therapeutic Considerations**
     Introduction 127
     The Physiology of Conception 131
     Therapeutic Solutions 141

IV. **New Ethical Issues**
    Introduction 175
    New Ethical Issues 177

V. Afterword 211

An Explanation of Rabbinic Terms 215

Contributors 219

INTRODUCTION

Lord Immanuel Jakobovits

The Biblical account of the human story begins with the imperative to "be fruitful and multiply" as the first of the Torah's 613 commandments. And Jewish history opens with the yearning to overcome the disability of childlessness. Abraham and Sarah were barren for most of their lives, to be granted the gift of a child only in hoary old age, while Rachel in her despair pleaded, "give me children or I am dead."

In Biblical times, only recourse to prayer and reliance on divine assurances could counter infertility. Today, thanks to the spectacular advances of medical science and technological skills, effective aids are available to triumph over many natural impediments, whether physical or psychological, on both the male and the female side.

But often these innovations raise new problems, particularly for observant and morally sensitive Jewish doctors and patients. Some of these difficulties may be of a purely religious or ritual character, such as possible clashes with the laws of family purity (*niddah*) when invasive procedures cause vaginal bleeding, or when treatments such as insemination or in vitro fertilization are required during the period of abstention. Other new techniques may encounter grave moral objections, such as when donated sperm or eggs are used to secure a successful impregnation. The resultant questions range from possibly violating the marriage bond by a quasi-adulterous relationship to establishing the true identity of a child born without certainty as to father, mother and other blood relatives.

Of course, Jewish teachings not only create problems; they often help to solve them. Lives sanctified by strict adherence to moral precepts tend to be superior lives, less prone to erosion of faithlessness, the alienation of children from their parents, or the subversion of society by indiscipline and selfishness.

This book — the first of its kind to deal specifically with infertility — provides an extensive survey of the relevant medical and halakhic data, based on professional expertise and the verdicts of many leading rabbinical authorities. Readers will be interested not only in their sometimes diverse rulings, but equally in the sources and thought processes leading to their conclusions.

Not least valuable, I hope, will be the deep concern of Judaism and its administrators to overcome the trials of infertility evinced in these papers, together with the encouragement given to persons who are perplexed or distressed.

May the children to be born out of the application of Jewish insights into the scientific wonders of modern medicine personify the intentions of this valuable volume's authors to increase life and to hallow it.

for my family,
   with love

FOREWORD

It has been my good fortune in life to be engaged in a calling which fulfills me and those whose paths cross mine, both at the same time. Helping a couple to build a family provides me with my greatest professional thrill, as those who have been on the receiving end have well understood. Still, I've no doubts about my role in all this. It is to be a proper *shaliach* (emissary) that I aspire.

It was with this in mind that I began putting this book together nearly five years ago. Although, at that time, my practice in reproductive medicine was only beginning to grow, it was already obvious that a text of this type would be helpful to many people. Technological advances in treating infertility were developing at an astounding pace, to the point where it seemed that nearly every clinical problem had a solution. Yet, within the traditional Jewish community, couples were largely unsure about the appropriateness of using this technology to their advantage. To make matters more complicated, their rabbinical advisors were often unclear about just what these treatments involved, and so they could offer no clear guidelines for approaching them. Physicians involved in treating these couples were typically uninformed about the restrictions under which these therapies could be offered.

My position as the Director of Reproductive Medicine at Maimonides Medical Center placed me in the center of these issues on a daily basis. The medical center is located in Boro Park, Brooklyn, home to one of the largest Orthodox Jewish communities in the world. In the surrounding neighborhoods, having children is not just a casual consequence of being married — it is a serious life calling. As a result, infertility is nothing less than a devastating illness. Against this scenario, my personal religious commitment, my familiarity with both the culture and language of halakha (Jewish law) and my practical knowledge of the medical issues involved together set me squarely in the middle of many a dramatic circumstance.

As we struggled to address the issues of the day, the important "players" in the clinical management of infertility began to define themselves. Requests for consultation came not only from patients but also from their rabbis. Conversations with the latter were often frustrating in that there were few, if any, precedents with which to address certain issues and, at the time, many were not yet part of the halakhic vocabulary. Many calls also came from my physician colleagues. And here, the following must be said: most fertility specialists are fervent about their work. They understand the magnitude of what they are doing and the consequences of success or failure for each couple. Naturally, therefore, there is great confusion about things that are highly feasible, seemingly ethical, yet impermissible for halakhically technical reasons.

The audience for this work is consequently a threefold one. For the rabbinic community, it contains basic information about reproductive physiology and the ways in which it can be manipulated in order to overcome infertility. A summary of recent halakhic discussions that have addressed the new reproductive technologies is also included and may serve as a basis for future problem-solving. For physicians who deal with Orthodox infertile couples, the chapter dealing with the basic laws of *niddah* (family purity) will likely be revealing and helpful in understanding some of the important issues that confront their patients. On a very practical level, strategies that can be used to keep fertility therapy within the guidelines of halakha are presented in detail. Rabbis and physicians will both benefit from reading the chapters on the special psychological and social problems faced by devout infertile couples.

It is my sincere hope that a greater familiarity with these issues will heighten the sensitivity that is shown infertile couples by those who care for them both physically and spiritually. On another level, my intention is that both professionals will recognize in this presentation not only the importance of their respective roles but also the boundaries to their areas of expertise. One of my goals in presenting this material is to clarify those boundaries and to encourage the rabbinic and medical community to interface more closely in assisting their common clients.

Of course, the third part of my intended audience is the most important one. Orthodox couples living within the halakhic community account for a large portion of my professional energy. It is for them that I have put this work together, expecting that in it they may find guidance and hope.

❑ ❑ ❑

This book is intended to cover the broadest possible spectrum within the traditional (halakhic) Jewish community. It is not intended to serve as a halakhic source, just as it is not intended to serve as a source of medical advice. It's purpose is to open up for all parties involved new dimensions to their labors. Ultimately, the material it presents should create better educated consumers as well as better informed caregivers.

Those who collaborated with me on this project have brought together a diverse experience with the problem of infertility in the traditional Jewish community. What has bound us together is the unusual fence which each of us has to straddle. That is, we continually see professionally interesting clinical problems on one side confront a strict set of religious mores on the other. Throughout the preparation of this work and, to a certain extent, throughout our careers, we remain perched on that fence. What we have gathered together is a description of some of the problems we face and some of the solutions that have emerged from our involvement.

Sara Barris and Joel Comet shared with me the conception of this book. In 1989, we led a workshop at a RESOLVE symposium which focused on the special problems of Orthodox couples. As each couple related the particulars of their personal despair, we were left feeling that something needed to be done. Together, we conceived of a book which would bring together the halakhic issues pertaining to infertility. Their chapter on the psychological and social problems that affect Jewish infertile couples is especially insightful and should be helpful not only to those couples but also to the physicians and rabbis who work with them.

There are numerous other individuals whom I would like to thank for helping me to put together this work. Lord Immanuel Jakobovits, the pioneer in presenting halakhic medical ethics to the broader community, was kind enough to write the introduction to this book. I am grateful for his interest.

Dr. Yoel Jakobovits presented the first essay, which was thorough in its scope and which set a scholarly tone for those that followed. This work has already appeared as a separate piece in *Tradition*, and I must acknowledge his patience in waiting to see it where it rightfully belongs. I would also like to thank the editors of *Tradition* for allowing me to reprint this material.

Like Dr. Jakobovits, Dr. Richard Weiss also combines the qualities of a *talmid hakham* (Torah scholar) and physician. His chapter on the laws of *niddah* is thoroughly detailed and referenced and should serve as essential reading for gynecologists who care for Orthodox women. He and I want to thank Rav Hershel Schachter, Rosh Kollel at Yeshiva University, for reviewing the material.

Rabbi Allen Schwartz contributed a thoughtful essay; his involvement with infertile couples and deep concern for them is obvious throughout. I must also thank Rabbi Heshie Billet, not only for the interesting analysis he provides in his chapter but also for his help in bringing the book to Genesis Jerusalem Press. Rabbi Jay Marcus of Genesis Jerusalem Press must also be thanked for the enthusiasm he has shown for this work and for all his assistance in turning my manuscript into a published book. My secretary, Maria Stuto, typed and retyped the manuscript many times; her gracious help with this and all aspects of my practice have been invaluable.

There is a tradition in Judaism of *hakarat hatov*, acknowledging a favor. This work would not have been possible without the many favors done for me by Dr. Joel B. Wolowelsky, who continues to be my teacher as well as my friend. His greatest favor has been his broadening of my contacts with scholars in the halakhic community. The perspective this has given me in my work has helped me in innumerable ways. Regarding this book, Joel was enthusiastic from its inception and encouraged me along the way. He was also the grand facilitator, about whom it can honestly be said that without his help, this work could not have been possible.

My wife, Leslie, bears the brunt of my long hours and the stresses that come with the professional undertakings that I have made. Her individuality, personal strengths and commitments have enabled me to meet those obligations. As my silent partner in all that I do, I publicly acknowledge my love and respect for her. May our children, Sally, Joseph, Ariel, Rebecca and Evan — and their children and grandchildren — be guided by the same spirit which has moved me to produce this work.

R.V.G.

I. The Religious Jewish Infertile Couple

INTRODUCTION

In examining the problem of infertility, it is easy to become consumed with the complex details of diagnosis and treatment. The enormous need to be successful is felt not only by the affected couple, but usually by the physician as well. Together, they tend to focus their energies on the correction of certain physical problems. While this makes sense vis-à-vis the ultimate plan, it should not preclude a discussion and evaluation of the couple's emotional status. Studies have repeatedly shown improved treatment outcomes in groups of patients who have received appropriate counseling. Certainly, the relief of stress can improve cyclic hormonal functioning in women and sexual functioning in men. The improved result may be due, as well, to those couples' ability to persist in therapy until the desired result is attained. No matter how highly functioning the couple appears to be or how straightforward their fertility problem, it behooves the couple and the physician to understand the psychological and social context within which the couple functions.

For the couple who is committed to halakha and who lives in a community of likeminded people, the emergence of a fertility problem presents special difficulties and challenges. In this section, we will examine some of these, with specific emphasis on their origins and possible solutions. The material presented should help couples who are experiencing infertility to define some of the feelings and reactions which they must confront. Perhaps more importantly, it may prompt those who care for them to understand them more completely. Specifically, there is a great need for physicians to be sensitized to the cultural and religious framework within which these couples are coping with their infertility. Likewise, rabbis and family members must be better attuned to the unique pressures — both physical and psychological — under which the couple is living. Especially when treatment is protracted, successful resolution of infertility is best acheived when patients, their caregivers and their counselors all understand these issues.

The Longing for Children in a Traditional Jewish Family

Yoel Jakobovits

Judaism regards the gift of children as one of life's preeminent endowments — and challenges. Fertility is among the most cherished of blessings, an attitude graphically amplified in Psalm 128 which speaks of "a wife as fruitful as a vine," whose "children are as olive plants around the table" leading to the ultimate joy of seeing "children to thy children." This is vividly emphasized by the belief[1] that there is a predestined number of people who must be born before the Messiah can come. Therefore, having more children hastens his arrival.

It has been postulated that the Jewish approach to procreation is, in addition, partially shaped by a legacy of lamentable historical conditions.[2] Frequent physical assault by massacres and pogroms coupled with equally devastating forced conversions and not-so-forced assimilation constitute an enormous — and, alas, persistent — depletion of Jewish demographics. A collective, subconscious instinct may exist to replenish these losses by achieving birth rates far in excess of the growth of the ambient society. Interesting and attractive as this theory is, its validity as a historically valid social force remains conjectural, the thesis as yet untested by comparing different Jewish communities in separate periods.

The most distinctive defining characteristic of the observant Jew is, of course, loyalty to the dictates of Jewish law. Though not the *only* reason for marriage,[3] bearing children fulfills three specific religious imperatives — and sets the stage for many others — and is therefore the quintessential ambition of a religious couple. Indeed, the primacy of the mitzvah of procreation is reflected in its being first in the Torah.[4] Actually, the Mishnah[5] regards the Biblical references in Genesis as merely requiring, as a minimum, the reproduction of the couple by having at least two children. However, the Talmud explicates two supplementary ordinances. One, of Biblical origin, known as *la-shevet*, is based on the verse in Isaiah 45:18: "Not for void did He create the world, but for habitation (*la-shevet*) did He form it." The second, of rabbinic derivation, is known as *la-erev* and is based on the verse: "In the morning, sow thy seed, and in the evening (*la-erev*) do not withhold your hand." Subsequently these precepts were codified by Maimonides: "Although a man has fulfilled the mitzvah of *p'ru ur'vu* (be fruitful and multiply), he is commanded by the Rabbis not to desist from procreation while he yet has strength, for whoever adds even one Jewish soul is considered as having created an entire world."[6]

The pressure, therefore, on devout Jewish infertile couples is often more intense than that which is found among the population at large. Indeed, the opposite calculations may pertain. Whereas a modern, secular couple might choose to "protect" themselves against pregnancy during their first few years of marriage, the Jewish allegiant couple yearns for early parenthood. Actually, both prototypes are motivated to solidify their as yet tenuous relationships. A secular couple may believe that the premature arrival of children would likely undermine their vulnerable ties. By contrast, the religiously inclined pair believes that early parenthood is more apt to cement their marital bonds through the commonality of offspring. These divergent positions can be traced to the fundamentally differing views of the marital covenant itself. On the one hand, many secular couples think of the *privileges* of marriage as paramount. On the other hand, the religiously sensitive couple regards marriage's *responsibilities* as preeminent. In other words, a secular view might emphasize the couple's fulfillment in one another; the religious view stresses their fulfillment in their offspring.

These sociologic features are ubiquitous in the religious Jewish community, fostering an unusual urgency to the resolution of infertility difficulties. It is common for childless couples to seek early counsel, perhaps even within the first few months of marriage. The urge to ignore such entreaties as premature must be tempered by the recognition that these cultural phenomena are deeply rooted in religious law and custom.

The mysterious[7] nature of the miracle of procreation instinctively prompts many infertile couples to first seek guidance and blessing from spiritual rather than medical sources. An ancient axiom states that "a blessing is only effective on that which is concealed from the eye."[8] The psychological sensitivity of intimate human relationships cannot be over-emphasized. Great care must be exercised in advising a couple to embark on the trail of infertility investigation. A precise recommendation as to how much time should elapse before infertility investigations are begun cannot be made. Although, by convention,[9] couples who remain childless after one year of regularly sexually active married life are called infertile, the point at which the diagnosis of infertility is earned is quite variable.

Regarding the "right time" at which to initiate the various stages of infertility testing, the rabbinic opinions differ. For example, while some[10] allow semen analysis only after ten years, others urge only a five[11] or even a two[12] year period. Rabbi Waldenberg[13] underscores the need to tailor one's approach to the individual cases at hand.

Even though the *halakha* may have no technical opposition to some investigations, there are some important psychological aspects to consider. The confirmation, particularly during the early months of marriage, by objective scientific testing, of testicular failure in the male or ovarian failure in the female can have a devastating impact on the affected partner and hence on the marriage itself. Consequently great deliberation must be exercised when acquiescing to — or counseling — a couple asking for fertility testing.

Recurrent spontaneous abortions — miscarriages — can have the same outcome as infertility, albeit with much greater psychological repercussions. Therefore, counseling in instances of miscarriage must be conducted with commensurately greater sympathy and understanding. In general, young couples ought to be dissuaded from immediately undertaking costly, intensive investigations. Rather, they should be informed that it is estimated that up to a third of all human pregnancies end in spontaneous losses. As an application of the concept of survival of the fittest, early spontaneous miscarriages can be viewed as nature's (that is, God's) way of culling out the most feeble fetuses. Couples ought to delay formal investigations at least until after two or even three consecutive spontaneous losses. Both the couple and their advisor should be aware that the earlier premature investigations are conducted, the greater the halakhic hurdles are likely to be.

We have already emphasized the degree to which an observant Jewish infertile couple may feel compelled to seek medical help. The couple will often first seek the guidance of their rabbi. Indeed, infertility difficulties, in particular, are associated with prayer and spiritual exertions. The very concept of supplication in prayer to the Creator has its roots in our nation's principal matriarchs, Sarah, Rebecca, and Rachel, all of whom were infertile through many years of marriage. The Bible chronicles their yearning for the blessing of children through anguished prayer, prompting the Rabbis to declare that "God is desirous of the prayer of the righteous."[14] These moving passages were eventually regarded as the paradigm of prayer and were therefore incorporated into the High Holiday services.[15] All who are involved in advising such people must be sensitive to these metaphysical aspects of their petitioner's needs.

10 BE FRUITFUL AND MULTIPLY

NOTES

1. Yevamot 62a, 63b; Avoda Zara 5b; Niddah 13b.
2. D.M. Feldman, *Marital Relations, Birth Control and Abortion in Jewish Law* (New York: Schocken Books, 1974), p.51.
3. See, for example, the series of expositions on the inherent value of marriage for the male partner in Yevamot 62b, where one who is unmarried is regarded as being without joy, blessing, good, Torah, protection, and peace. Likewise the Talmud (Yevamot 118b; Kiddushin 7a, 41a) often assumes that marriage is beneficial for the female partner: *"Tav l'metav tan du mi-l'metav armelu* — It is always to her advantage to be part of a tandem, married, rather than alone." Both references focus on the companionship, non-procreative aspects of marriage.
4. Rashi and Tosafot, Yevamot 65b; Nahmanides, Genesis 9:7 hold that the verses addressed to the Noahidic survivors of the Flood (ibid. 9:1, 7) and to Jacob (ibid. 35:11) are the source of this injunction. Contrary to the common assumption, the charge to Adam and Eve (ibid. 1:28) is actually a blessing, not a commandment.
5. Yevamot VI, 6 (61b).
6. Yad HaHazaka, Hilkhot Ishut 15:16.
7. E.E. Wallach, "The Enigma of Unexplained Infertility," *Postgrad Obst Gyn* 5:1 (1985) alludes to some of these unexplained phenomena. In general, it emphasizes, that the shorter the duration of infertility, the better the associated prognosis.
8. Ta'anit 8b; Bava Metziah 42a. In fact several studies highlight the fact that pregnancy rates are fairly independent of treatment! See, for example, J.A. Collins, W. Wrixon, L.B. Jones, E.H. Wilson, "Treatment-In-

dependent Pregnancy Among Infertile Couples," *New Engl J Med* 309:1201 (1983).
9. See note 7. It should be noted that the authors report that 64% to 79% of women with infertility will conceive within nine years. Clearly, however, investigations should not be delayed until the
10. Resp. Minhat Yitzhak, 3:108.
11. Resp. Iggrot Moshe, Even HaEzer, 2:16.
12. Hazon Ish cited by A. Avraham's Nishmat Avraham, Even HaEzer 23:2, p. 113.
13. Resp. Tzitz Eliezer IX 51:1.2.
14. Yevamot 64a.
15. The Torah reading for the first day of Rosh Hashanah, taken from Bereshit 21, recounts the realization of Sarah's plea upon the birth of Isaac. Similarly, the Haftarah (I Samuel 1 and 2) relates how Hannah was ultimately blessed with the birth of Samuel. The Talmud (Megillah 31a) tells us that Sarah and Hannah were both remembered on Rosh Hashanah.

THE RABBINIC AND MEDICAL PARTNERSHIP

Heshie Billet

Rav Joseph B. Soloveitchik once observed that Jews must function in two dimensions. On the one hand, we share the universal human condition with all of mankind. On the other, we must confront life in our own unique, particularistic way. The instinct and ability to reproduce was implanted in mankind at the time of creation, and from this perspective Jews share with non-Jews the common problems associated with infertility. At the same time, though, we have our own religious rules relating to our Biblical, prophetic and rabbinic sources defining our special commandment to "be fruitful and fill the earth."

For a traditional Jewish couple, infertility is both a medical and a religious problem. As a medical problem, it requires the services of medical practitioners and the assistance of emotional support groups or professionals. As a religious problem, it requires a rabbinic consultation for clarification of halakhic and ethical issues which might be associated with each particular case.

Despite the fact that couples facing a problem of infertility are most often in good health, from a halakhic perspective infertility is a medical problem which is included under the license to heal that the halakha has given physicians.

The Bible includes many narratives, from the times of the Patriarchs through the times of the prophets, concerning couples who had difficulty conceiving children. From the perspective of the Bible and the Talmud (Yevamot 64a), prayer is seen as a solution to this problem. God is the Creator, the source of life, and He holds the keys to conception (Ta'anit 2a). Rebecca, Isaac and Hannah all succeeded through their prayers and were blessed with children. Judaism accepts that the metaphysical world directly affects the physical world. Therefore, prayer, an instrument of the metaphysical world, is seen as a means through which people can be helped to have children. Indeed when the Rabbis formulated the daily essential prayer, they included a blessing for health. Prayer, then, is a vehicle which is designed to assist people in overcoming physical, health related problems. Included in this category are problems related to procreation.

The "License to Heal" and its Relationship to Infertility

Talmudic and rabbinic sources cite numerous precedents for allowing a physician to engage in the practice of medicine, with the goal of assisting people in overcoming their medical problems. In the following paragraphs, we will analyze the different sources on this subject and see how they lend themselves to the medical treatment of infertility.

The Talmud (Bava Kama 85a) uses the verse "And he shall cause him to be thoroughly healed" (Exodus 21:19) as the source for a doctor's license to cure. Rashi and Tosafot both indicate that this license is necessary so that medical assistance not be seen as a human effort attempting to circumvent divine decrees. The Midrash Temurah further develops the point that medical practice should be seen as an element of the partnership established between God and man in enhancing the quality of life in the world. Man is expected to fertilize, to plant, to harvest, to build, and to heal, to make God's world a better place in which to live. Maimonides, in his commentary on the Mishnah (Pesahim 4:10) sees man's search for medical help as a form of *bitahon*, trust in God. From this point of view, the work of physicians who assist couples in their effort to conceive children certainly fulfills the stipulations of the divine mission of medical practice.

Furthermore, the Talmud declares that if any human being saves a single soul in Israel, it is regarded as if he had saved an entire world (Sanhedrin 37a). Although this statement refers to saving a life that already exists, it might be applied to assisting the birth of unborn or not yet conceived children as well. Certainly, we believe that the destiny of Israel is bound with those not yet born as well as those already alive (Deuteronomy 29:14, Yevamot 62a).

Another source for the physician's license to practice is the verse in Leviticus (19:16), "You shall not stand idly by the blood of your neighbor." Rav Yosef Karo (Shulhan Arukh, Yoreh De'ah 336:1) says that the physician as a healer saves lives, and withholding care is considered to be the shedding of blood. Rashi (Genesis 16:2) says that someone without children is considered devastated and the Talmud (Nedarim 64b) considers such a person to be without life. From this perspective, a physician who helps people to conceive is considered a restorer of life to the parents of the child.

Maimonides (Commentary on the Mishnah, Nedarim 4:4) sees the physician's responsibility to his patients as a function of the Biblical verse which requires us to restore lost property, "And you shall restore it to him" (Deuteronomy 22:2). A person whose reproductive system needs medical intervention to restore it to proper function would fall under this category.

Nahmanides declares that the physician's medical practice is mandated by "Love your neighbor as yourself" (Leviticus 19:18). The implication of this commandment broadens the role of the physician to include other acts of kindness beyond healing. Hence, even if one were to argue that people who have a fertility problem are not technically ill, the physician would nevertheless be obligated to assist those people.

There are several other halakhic issues which might be raised by medical treatment for infertility. Does such treatment apply equally to a woman and a man, inasmuch as a woman is not commanded to fulfill the mitzvah of procreation? From the perspective of "love your neighbor," it might be argued that there is no difference between a man and a woman. A female who yearns for a child is suffering both physically and emotionally. "Love your neighbor" requires that we reach out to the woman as well. From the perspective of being devastated without children and having life restored with children, it would seem that there is no difference between a man and a woman. Indeed, Sarah is the Biblical source of the notion of childless persons being devastated, as she declared, "Perhaps I will be rebuilt from her." A woman whose reproductive system needs repair would seem to fit the stipulations of "you shall restore it...."

Another question might relate to the form of the therapy. Risky, experimental, and non-therapeutic procedures pose halakhic questions. Percentage of success and consequences of failed treatment are all factors which have to be weighed according to different authorities. Also to be considered is that some authorities might not see infertility as a life threatening circumstance. Despite Talmudic sources which suggest such an analogy, in reality infertility is not really a physical threat to life and limb. The majority point of view would encourage couples to seek help. Yet it is important to understand the nature of all forms of treatment to assure that they do not contradict halakha.

A Note of Caution

Once it has been established halakhically that the medical community plays an important role in assisting couples along the road to parenthood, we must define the parameters within which that community may function in helping a traditional Jewish couple. If physicians or counselors wish to properly serve their religious patients, then they must accept that not all of the secular or ethical norms of their profession are acceptable to those patients. The professional must recognize that a local rabbi and/or halakhic authority may have to be consulted to help the couple resolve certain moral and halakhic issues which might arise in treating their problem. The physician/counselor must realize that, for these patients, resolving these questions in a halakhic way is as important as having a satisfactory result from their treatment. The infertility practitioner should therefore be sensitive to the patient's needs and interact in a positive manner with the patient's rabbi, deferring to him in halakhic matters.

The rabbi, on the other hand, has to be realistic about his role as well. Often, a religious couple will consult with their rabbi before seeking medical advice. The rabbi should be aware of the limitations of his role and should not try to dispense medical advice. Rather, a knowledgeable rabbi should see his relationship to the couple as a supportive one. The rabbi should know when the couple's fears are premature and when they are timely. He should be prepared to advise the couple about the relevant halakhic issues and should interact with the physician accordingly.

In summary, the appropriate treatment for the fertility problem of a traditional Jewish couple requires the interface of the medical community with the religious community. Such cooperative interactions would serve the couple in a positive way and hopefully will result in the "whole" patient being treated with sensitivity and dignity.

INFERTILITY:
ISSUES FROM THE HEART

Sara Barris and Joel Comet

In our years of working with infertile individuals, couples and their families, we have frequently heard these typical questions and comments: A parent-in-law asks, "Why are they making such a big deal about this? Thank God, it's not cancer. God will surely help!" A women a year into her infertility diagnosis bemoans, "Why do I feel like every time I come up for air, I'm drowning again?" A man five years into his infertility questions, "Why can't I get on with my life? It feels like everything is on hold!"

 For an outsider looking in, it is difficult to get a sense of what it is like to go through infertility. For those going through the ordeal, it is often a shock to see just how profoundly infertility disrupts their lives. Much has been written to shed light on why infertility has such a far-reaching impact.[1] The impact reflects the reality that infertility is a life crisis which permeates one's sense of self, one's marriage, one's relationship with extended family, one's relationship with community, and finally, one's relationship with God. In this essay, we will focus on how these issues are intensified for the Orthodox infertile couple.

There are two unique aspects in the interplay between infertility and Orthodoxy that make it a different experience from other medical illnesses. First, for those who are Orthodox, infertility directly challenges the first commandment, "*p'ru ur'vu* (be fruitful and multiply)." This commandment has become one of the most pivotal and precious values in Jewish life, that of building a family. Child-free living is not as viable an option as it might be for couples without this religious commitment.

Second, in traditional Jewish thought, the values of modesty, privacy, and a special sense of "holiness" surround the body parts and physical behaviors involved with reproduction. These are suddenly thrown open to widespread scrutiny by physicians and to speculation by the community. It often requires a long and difficult transition for Orthodox couples to begin to deal with infertility issues more openly and comfortably. If they are unable to negotiate this transition, they may slowly withdraw from friends and community. The couple is often left lacking in knowledge and experiencing feelings of embarrassment and shame.

In the sections below, we will expand on the critical challenges that confront the Orthodox infertile couple and their family.

Personal

As we grow and mature, all of us anticipate and prepare for the roles we are to play in life. These roles are derived from general culture and society and are accentuated by our religious beliefs and practices. Whatever other professional or social roles women see themselves playing in society, being a mother remains an integral part of a religious woman's female identity. It is a role girls practice for and fantasize about from childhood onward. No woman expects to be infertile. If she is, her predicament forces her to question her basic sense of self: What does it mean to be a woman who may not bear children? What does it mean to be a wife who may not be able to be a mother? As she is challenged to redefine the roles she has accepted and prepared for so long, new role definitions are not readily available. Such a woman may suddenly find herself in a state of limbo.

When an observant woman gets married, she thinks about starting a family and, accordingly, makes critical decisions about other aspects of her life, such as continuing secular or religious education, accepting job offers or pursuing a career. With infertility and the reawakening of the question of role definition, all of these decisions need to be thought through again. However, new roles and plans become difficult to pursue due to both logistical and emotional factors. The unpredictability, time and effort involved in infertility treatment may require a woman to be available on specific days of her cycle, and at short notice. The emotional upheaval of infertility may make it difficult to focus on other facets of her life. As one woman put it: "I'm miserable at my job, but how can I concentrate on looking for new possibilities when all my time and energy is consumed by my infertility?" Such a woman is left feeling empty; she is not a mother and she is too depleted to enhance and develop other parts of her identity.

Men frequently report that infertility attacks their sense of self on many levels. The Torah clearly defines a man's role in the context of his family. It is the man who has the religious obligation to reproduce and it is he who is expected to take on the responsibility as provider for his wife's material and sexual needs. The infertile man may doubt his ability to be an effective husband. He may believe that he is disappointing his wife and feel like a failure. Moreover, secular society shapes men's attitudes with messages that equate sexual performance with manhood. Male infertility is often mistakenly equated with physical impotence by the naive general public. Even infertile men who function well sexually may make that equation on an emotional level. They end up feeling like they are not "really men" and are often engulfed in a pervasive, vague sense of shame. A husband may begin to think that perhaps his wife would have been better off marrying somebody else. In addition, the religious man may be plagued by the thought that he cannot fulfill his religious obligation to reproduce.

The role of a father in relation to his child is also clearly defined and structured in religious society. A fundamental task is teaching one's children Torah. The childless Orthodox man is constantly reminded of his inability to fulfill this Torah mandate. When he attends Sabbath services, he feels empty as he is surrounded by other fathers praying alongside their children. As he builds his *sukkah*, he cannot help but notice that other men around him are aided by all their children. When he lights Hannuka candles, he is pained at being unable to share the blessings. At the Passover Seder, he yearns to hear a small voice asking him the Four Questions. On Shavuot he craves to teach a child of his own during his all-night studies. Being unable to fulfill these expected roles of husband and father often leaves men feeling incomplete and anguished.

An integral part of a religious perspective is the value that is placed on constant improvement of one's character traits. It can be very difficult to feel that one is embracing this value in the face of the wide range of powerful emotions that are experienced and reexperienced at different stages of the infertility process. Anger, guilt, shame, depression, grief and jealousy are all common feelings that anyone going through infertility experiences, yet people are frequently shocked at their presence and their power. They would never believe themselves capable of harboring these feelings, which can seem so unacceptable at times, such as when one feels jealous and angry about one's close friend becoming pregnant. As these feelings arise, so does the guilt around one's failure to maintain a virtuous character. Many individuals feel that they are alone in experiencing these feelings and that these emotions reflect their own poor character. This leaves them feeling unworthy, isolated and out of control.

Anger, which is often close to the surface and frequently directed at one's spouse, friends, family members and doctors — all of whom may be less than perfectly sensitive — can be very unsettling. It may be directed at one's spouse for letting one down or for not being supportive. It is often directed at friends and relatives for failing to understand and for making well-intentioned but hurtful comments, such as, "You know, you're not getting any younger!" or,

"Your poor sister, she just gave birth and had such a hard labor!" It may be felt towards physicians for not being successful, for building up expectations, for running their offices like factories, or for making their insensitive comments, such as, "You're ruining my statistics!" It may also be directed at oneself as each individual searches out reasons to explain why he or she has been "punished" with this affliction.

Rather than berating themselves for experiencing these feelings, individuals must recognize that these feelings are common and normal. Even the Torah accepts these feelings as valid. For example, Rachel was jealous of her sister Leah, and Hannah, who was to become mother to the prophet Samuel, was inconsolably depressed. The Midrash recognizes these feelings as being positively motivated and acceptable. This does not mean that people are encouraged to immerse themselves and drown in their feelings. Rather, they should not berate themselves for having these feelings and thus enter a cycle of self-blame which will further intensify the painful feelings. Acknowledging these feelings helps the person gain a sense of validity and allows one to begin the process of letting go and moving on.

Resolving the emotions evoked by infertility is a process that takes place over time. Resolution does not mean that feelings will never emerge again, even if couples are successful at having biological children. Like any wound that heals, it is more readily opened at vulnerable times in one's life, such as when one loses a family member. When healthy resolution begins to occur, couples can experience inner growth and strength of character. There can be increased sensitivity to others and the ability to be less judgmental about other peoples' apparent negative behavior. One knows firsthand that surface behaviors do not necessarily reflect what the person is going through and one is better able to fulfill the traditional dictum of judging one's friend to his or her benefit.

It is not always easy to acknowledge these feelings as normal, especially when they relate to God. Many people question, "Why is God punishing me? Am I so bad? Am I that much worse than the next person?" This is particularly difficult for people who became observant later in life and who feel that they have made tremendous effort to elevate their religious functioning. It is often difficult and frightening for individuals to question and doubt God's justice, especially when these doubts are mixed with feelings of anger and fear of punishment. The traditional Jewish view that nothing in life is accidental can sometimes provide comfort. Using the models of our Patriarchs and Matriarchs who struggled with infertility, one can bring these difficult feelings into prayers to God. Many rabbis recommend that prayer for oneself and others and involvement in charitable activities can bring one closer to God and minimize feelings of alienation.

Profound feelings of grief and depression may occur and are often misunderstood by friends and family. It may be hard to understand the depth of these feelings because they are grieving for something vague, invisible and potential. Couples may be grieving for many different types of losses: the unborn child, the pregnancy experience, sharing the birth experience with each other, bringing up a child steeped in Torah and good deeds, their own mortality or the inability to compensate for the losses of the

Holocaust with their own biological children. The loss may be different for each spouse. It is important for each partner to empathically understand both their own and their spouse's experience. Judaism does not provide rituals for mourning these losses. Couples are left to mourn these losses on their own without guidelines and structures that are available for other types of losses, such as *shiva* and *kaddish*. It may be helpful for couples to mark these losses for themselves by giving to a special charity, by setting aside a special Torah topic to learn together or by otherwise developing their own meaningful expressions of their grief.

Marriage

Unfortunately, the effects of infertility do not remain with the individual but permeate his or her relationships with others. A frequent casualty is the marriage. The marital relationship requires an enormous amount of energy, attention and nurturing to keep it refueled from the constant draining demands that are placed on it. Many Orthodox couples begin trying to conceive immediately after they get married. These young relationships, without the benefit of a maturational process, are particularly vulnerable. In more mature relationships, communication skills have been improved, intimacy has deepened and empathy has grown, thus better preparing the couple to deal with stressful events. Couples who decided (with or without rabbinic approval) to postpone trying to conceive until later in their marriage may need to deal with a sense of guilt for having waited.

Newly married couples who are just beginning to learn to know one another and become comfortable with one another on a physically intimate level can easily feel overwhelmed. Their sexual relationship becomes subject to scrutiny by themselves, doctors, nurses, lab staff and indirectly by parents, in-laws, extended family and community (who may be wondering why the couple is not pregnant). At times, it feels that this process removes the "holiness" and intimacy from marital relations and leaves in its place a mechanical and dehumanizing act.

For many couples, the spontaneity and intimacy of sexual relations is compromised by medical procedures which dictate the exact day and time of intercourse. The laws of *niddah* that relate to a woman's menstrual cycle intensify these issues for the Orthodox couple. At a minimum, twelve days out of every monthly cycle is sexually off limits for the couple. On top of that, fertility therapy often further restricts the halakhicly permissible time that a couple can be physically intimate with one another. A treatment procedure can cause a woman to become *niddah*, thereby prohibiting physical relations for at least an additional seven days. A doctor may instruct a couple to abstain from relations in order to increase the potency of the sperm or direct the couple to abstain until the woman is ovulating, which can be several days after the couple could otherwise halakhicly engage in sexual relations.

The infertility treatment turns marital relations into a pressured, conflicting and often unsatisfying experience. The Orthodox couple is left with very few days to engage in relaxed physical intimacy. Instead of physical intimacy nurturing the young marriage, the marital relationship is depleted.

Donor insemination is a controversial halakhic

issue, and couples choosing this as a treatment option have to deal with additional complex issues evoking feelings of disloyalty and betrayal. Wives may feel "violated" while husbands may feel estranged.

The complexity and high-tech nature of fertility treatments raise many halakhic issues which require a couple to consult a rabbi. These questions have become very complicated and require a halakhic authority who is knowledgeable and informed in this area. Even given this expertise, there is a range of different viewpoints, and tensions may occur in the relationship when a couple disagrees on whom to follow.

Rabbinic approval, as well as the family and community outlook, is also involved in the parenting options available to the couple. Rabbis differ in the degree to which they encourage adoption or donor insemination as viable options, and communities differ in the level of acceptance or stigma they apply to it.

These additional complexities confronting Orthodox couples can lead them to feel misunderstood and alienated from one another. Some couples may react to this by building barriers between themselves. Other couples may experience increased levels of stress and animosity, and may fight more. Each spouse may end up feeling more alone and fragile. It is therefore especially important for them to make a conscious effort to develop ways of being mutually sympathetic and supportive. One way of coping is to learn when one's spouse is particularly vulnerable and to take turns at being the stronger one, such as at the onset of the menstrual period, the pregnancy of a close relative or the day when sperm has to be tested. Husband and wife may find that they react differently to their infertility. They may experience the losses differently and have different ways of coping. It is helpful to place themselves in their spouse's shoes and understand the loss experience from their spouse's point of view. (An excellent couples exercise is to switch roles and see if one can accurately express one's spouse's feelings.) It also helps to share the burden of gathering and understanding the medical information so that one spouse does not feel overwhelmed while the other feels excluded. Couples should not choose one spouse to hear a doctor's recommendations and treatment plans. It is important to keep in mind that no matter which spouse is experiencing the primary medical problem or emotional reaction, infertility is always a couple's shared issue. When handled with care and sensitivity, the pain and trauma of infertility can ultimately bring couples closer together and help them to develop a solid and loving marriage.

Family

Although families are traditional sources of support and comfort during crises, couples suffering from infertility often feel a further strain from their family. As mentioned above, modesty discourages people from discussing issues relating to their sexual relationship. Despite the fact that infertility is not a sexual issue per se, its association with marital relations can make it difficult and embarrassing to talk about. The intensity of emotions experienced — depression, anger, guilt, shame and embarrassment— can also lead the couple to withdraw into themselves and away from support systems. When one spouse would like to seek the support of extended family but the other feels too ashamed to do so, marital tensions are heightened. This lack of communication and information exchange may lead to comments that are well-intentioned by the extended family but interpreted as hurtful by the couple. For example: "Is there a sexual problem?" "What's taking so long?" "You're too tense! If you would just relax, you'd get pregnant." Parents of infertile couples must also deal with difficult feelings. They may feel intense sadness about the pain and suffering of their children. Self-blame and guilt can emerge as parents try to make sense of their children's infertility. Parents are also mourning the potential loss of their own grandchildren. Some families feel comfortable and encouraging of adoption as a way of building a family. For others, the importance of family genealogy makes adoption a more difficult choice. Overall, these difficulties experienced by the couple and their parents can create new barriers between them. As a result, the couple is left isolated and without a natural source of support. The extended family, for its part, may be left not knowing how to respond.

These kinds of issues may also occur for couples who have a child. Those who attained parenthood through donor insemination are usually secretive due to the stigma associated with it. They may feel unsupported and distressed when people assume that their infertility problem is resolved. For those suffering from so-called secondary infertility, the pain may be trivialized by others who make comments such as, "At least you have one child; you should be thankful."

Often, the infertile couple experiences rejection

when siblings with children are perceived as being overvalued by their parents. For example, parents may spend more time at the homes of sons and daughters who have children; they may talk about how much pleasure they get from their grandchildren. The infertile couple may experience pain when the family gets together around holiday times or celebrations such as a *brit* or *bat mitzvah*. These milestones, which traditionally serve to bring families together, end up leaving the couple with feelings of isolation, emptiness and estrangement.

Many couples are children of survivors of the Holocaust. There is a message embodied in that experience that it is important to compensate for the losses of the Holocaust and to ensure the continuity of the Jewish chain. The infertile couple may thus feel additional pressure or guilt for not being able to achieve this goal.

Couples and families can take steps to bring themselves closer together. The couples can be aware that their parents are also struggling with painful feelings. They need to assess what kind of emotional support they can realistically expect from their parents. Couples can educate and sensitize extended family members and let them know that they do not need to offer solutions or try to ease the pain with "helpful" advice. Just listening is often the most useful way to be supportive. Couples can encourage family members to read the literature on the emotional impact of infertility or attend workshops that will make them more aware of these issues. It is not uncommon for family members to attend these workshops, even independent of the infertile couple. When couples are considering other options, like adoption, they can help other family members by introducing the idea gradually and not springing it on them. Family members do not need to wait for the couple to offer information, but can make independent efforts to educate themselves about infertility and adoption. The ability of couples and their families to feel more comfortable with each other and with the issues of infertility is something that can take time to develop. When this process is worked on actively, it promotes connections, concern, and warmth that can be an anchor for the drifting, isolated couple.

Communal

Infertility also strikes out at our social relationships and involvement with community events. Reminders of one's childlessness are built into the religious communal aspects of our lives.

The synagogue used to be a place to relax and enjoy the joy of Sabbath. Now it has become a weekly reminder of how set apart the infertile members are from the rest of their peers. Synagogues are filled with children and pregnant women who enjoy discussing childbirth and child-rearing issues. The child-oriented festivals like Simhat Torah, Hannuka, Purim and Pesah make it painful for the infertile couple to participate, which leads to an increasing sense of isolation. One couple expressed their pain humorously: "We have no difficulty with the Jewish Holidays, we just pack up and go to Florida!" Other rituals present their own dilemmas. Being chosen to carry in the infant at a *brit* is traditionally supposed to bring good luck in having children. While some infertile couples appreciate the gesture, at the same time this honor singles out the infertile couple in the public eye and is a painful reminder of their infertility. Couples should realize that they do not have to accept every invitation to, and honor at, social or religious events that may be painful for them. Alternatively, they may agree beforehand to attend but then leave as soon as it becomes too difficult for either one to handle. A prearranged signal, a wink or gesture, and a prearranged excuse for leaving might be helpful. Couples can also role-play with each other the ways of responding to anticipated questions and comments about their situation.

In observant communities, where couples conceive soon after marriage, infertile couples soon become out of step with their peers. Close friends with whom they may have shared life-stage tasks and issues are now moving on and are consumed with discussions of a *brit*, diapers, childcare, schools and the like. Infertile couples find they have less and less in common with their friends. The turmoil of emotions they experience in social settings — embarrassment, jealousy, resentment — leads them to keep things in. The combination of having and sharing fewer common experiences, along with the difficult emotions evoked, places a strain on the continuity of meaningful relationships. Yet it is vital to avoid isolation and to receive appropriate social support. This does not mean having to share all the details of one's experience. Nevertheless, it is helpful to choose a close friend who has shown sensitivity in the past and to educate these confidants. Let them know that rather than offering advice, listening is often the best they can do. Simply listening may seem like insufficient help, but a sensitive friend who can empathize is providing a priceless means of support.

Interventions and Summary

As described above, infertility is an all-consuming crisis that pervades and disrupts multiple aspects of one's life experience. It is critical for infertile couples to develop coping skills and support systems to help deal with issues concerning themselves, their marriages, and their relationships with family, friends, and community.

It is easy to become absorbed by the emotional and medical aspects of infertility. Couples must actively develop and nurture other real and potential aspects of themselves and their relationships. Carving out time alone and with one another to pursue rewarding activities that have nothing to do with infertility provides a welcome and necessary safe haven. These "vacations" can vary from taking a weekend away to spending a half hour a day pursuing a relaxing activity.

Reaching out and connecting to others is probably the most significant action that the infertile couple can take to help themselves cope in more positive and productive ways. This includes connecting to family, friends, and other infertile couples. Specifically, connecting with others going through the infertility experience helps one feel less alone and may strengthen one's resolve. Connecting with the infertile community can be done in a number of ways, such as talking on an anonymous hotline with a volunteer or joining a peer group or support group with others sharing the experience. Contrary to popular misconceptions, well-run support groups do not suggest that people sit around encouraging one another to drown in self-pity. Rather, they offer an opportunity for people to share their feelings and experiences, to learn from one another's coping skills, and to find strength. Support groups provide the unique chance to offer strength to others. The goal that is reached is that people move forward in their lives in a more positive and productive way. For those who need an extra boost to help them get through a rough period, individual or marital counseling with a therapist experienced in this area can make a critical difference. These options are available through RESOLVE, INC., a non-profit, self-help infertility organization that dispenses medical information and moral support. Hooking up with self-help organizations also provides information about the latest medical techniques and quality of infertility specialists. Networking allows one to be more in control of one's self, one's situation, and one's medical treatment. Being more knowledgeable about treatments and treatment options allows couples to be more assertive with their physicians and to be able to pursue their treatments in a more productive manner.

Infertility treatment can go on for years. It is important for couples to periodically reevaluate their situation. This is not to forget their goal of becoming parents, but so that they can reserve their energy to pursue other credible options in parenting. Signs that will help a couple know that it is time to engage in this evaluation include: pursuing techniques over and over again despite low odds of a successful pregnancy resulting; ingesting large amounts of medication and ignoring potential side effects; depleting financial resources; and/or depleting emotional resources. It is not an easy decision to stop infertility treatments, especially in the light of tempting, newly emerging high-technology treatments which seem to offer that one last hope. In reality, for many, these treatments offer low odds and are expensive and time consuming.

To say that one must emotionally resolve one's infertility before pursuing other options is erroneous. Resolving the emotional aspects of infertility is a lifelong process that even the success of having biological children does not erase. Therefore, one can begin to explore other options even before one is ready to pursue them. This is especially true for couples who find that they are at different stages in looking at options. For many, foster-care, adoption, or volunteering with children is part of the resolution process. Couples can attend pre-adoption workshops even before they make a commitment. Some people pursue medical treatment following adoption with renewed energy; others feel ready to leave the treatments behind them. Couples can derive strength from looking at other families and learning how they have coped with infertility and overcome their obstacles.

Judaism holds that events are not accidental or random. It becomes the challenge of those confronted with adversity to use these experiences as a catalyst for positive and meaningful development as a Jew. The Talmud explains that our Patriarchs' and Matriarchs' infertility was due to God's desire to bring them closer to Him. The struggles and suffering of infertility can lead to growth of one's self, one's marriage and one's sensitivity to others. It is the individual's opportunity to translate this growth into an increased awareness of and involvement in *mitzvot*. This is both on a personal level (between man and God) and an interpersonal level — reaching out to others in need (between man and man). It is in this way of viewing our life events that we bring increased meaning and inspiration to our lives.

1. B.E. Menning, *Infertility: A Guide for the Childless Couple* (New York: Prentice Hall Press, 1988).

A RABBINIC RESPONSE TO INFERTILITY

Allen Schwartz

Procreation is the human's way of acting in partnership with God to actually imitate His creation of man.[1] It is the first commandment of the Torah[2] and, as the author of *Sefer Hahinukh* explains,[3] "[t]his is a great commandment by whose reason and means all other commandments are established."[4] Yet some people are unable to become parents. How does Judaism teach such people to come to terms with their infertility? Is infertility God's will? If God commanded the human race to procreate, why does He make procreation impossible for some people?

Of course, this is a general question that religious people must face on a regular basis. God commands us to give charity, but suddenly our finances turn sour and we cannot fulfill God's will. Every fall, we prepare to fulfill God's will that we eat in a *sukkah*; often He brings rain to frustrate our ability to fulfill this mitzvah. Somehow, we believe that the financial turn and the bad weather are part of God's plan for us and the world in which we live. We believe that only God knows why each event must take place and, in the course of life, we understand that fulfilling God's will takes a back seat to being part of God's plan.

God's will is that each and every human be fruitful and multiply. Yet, in the scheme of God's plan there may be an external design in which a person's inability to procreate will produce something positive, such as bringing an adopted child into one's family, teaching others about sensitivity to the human condition, or being inspired to write these feelings for the public. This is the essence of Nahum Ish Gamzu's Talmudic dictum, *"Gam zu l'tova* (this too is for good)."[5] Nahum, when faced with impending death, did not say *"Gam zu tova* (this too is good)," because death is not good. He said, rather, this too is *for* good, meaning I feel confident that this event will have some positive outcome. One need not deny the negative aspect of a situation in order to see that it may also have a positive result.

An infertile person must not see his condition as a punishment from God. We understand the Talmud's exhortation to "analyze one's deeds to determine the cause for suffering"[6] to mean that one should analyze what one may learn from suffering. How can one improve his or her own life as well as the lives of others based on adverse circumstances? How can one get close to his or her spouse though this? When the rabbis of the Talmud and Midrash noted the infertility of the Patriarchs and Matriarchs, they explained that God wanted to elicit the prayers of the righteous,[7] not that their suffering was due to some sin on their part.[8] One thing is clear: one may not explain the suffering of another; to do so is to violate the Torah prohibition of verbal oppression. If a person suffers from tragedy or illness, no one may presume to attribute the suffering to sins. It is not for humans to undertake a direct correlation between one's behavior and God's actions.[9]

Let us return to the analogy of the *sukkah*. The Talmud relates that when the nations of the world asked for a mitzvah, God granted them the mitzvah of sitting in the *sukkah*.[10] While sitting in their *sukkah*, the sun beat down on them so strongly that they were forced to leave. Upon leaving, they knocked down the *sukkah* in anger over being unable to perform the mitzvah. The Talmud reflects that according to *halakha* they were justified in leaving the *sukkah*; they were wrong for expressing their anger the way they did and thereby forfeited their ability to perform the commandment again. The message of this story is clear: If one is really interested in fulfilling God's will, one cannot be angry when God's plan interferes with one's ability to do so. If we are, we frustrate our ability to fulfill His will in the future.

In the twentieth century, so many options are open to infertile couples that were not available to previous generations. Our patriarchs and matriarchs had prayer and were quite successful at it. Today, medical advances can combine with prayer to serve as a powerful solution to this problem. The question we must answer is the extent of our *obligation* to do so. In other words, is an infertile couple halakhicly *required* to seek medical help in assisting conception?

This question perhaps also can be approached through the same analogy of the *sukkah*. The Mishnah[11] compared raining on the *sukkah* to a master pouring wine in his servant's face after the servant poured it for him. If the servant pours an additional cup, would not the master be incensed? In our situation, if God prevented a person from procreating — if it is part of God's plan that some *not* have children — who is that person to thwart God's plan? But the point is that we do not know God's plan. Perhaps the plan is that one should work *harder* to parent a child for a reason only God knows. When we *can* help ourselves, we ought to. In the case of rain in the *sukkah*, perhaps we can suggest that if there were some way for us to alter the rain on the holiday of Sukkot, we also ought to. However, there is no reason to say that we would *have* to do so. Procreation is a positive commandment, and positive commandments must be observed only to the point of dispensing with up to 20% of one's assets.[12] Putting oneself in harm's way would certainly be considered to be beyond a 20% dispensation of assets.[13] However, if one wants to do so, one certainly may.[14]

The fact that the Jewish community is family-centered can add to the emotional difficulties of the infertile couple. Rabbis are bound to deliver one or two sermons a year about the centrality of children in the synagogue and the community. Friends and family are bound to needle couples who remain childless after three or four years of marriage.

Talmudic and Midrashic sources refer directly to the relationship between the barren Hannah and her husband Elkanah's second wife Penina, who had children. Penina made Hannah's life miserable, taunting her that the Lord had closed her womb. Elkanah said to her, "Hannah, why are you crying and why aren't you eating? Why are you so sad? Am I not more devoted to you than ten sons?"[15] Some rabbinic sources maintain that Penina had good intentions and only meant to push Hannah to action.[16] However, one source[17] indicates that Penina would dress and wash her children and parade them before Hannah. She would take them to school and feed them in front of Hannah and gloat over her bounty.[18] The rabbis considered Penina's behavior so reprehensible as to warrant the death of all her children. Indeed, a remarkable passage from *Sefer Hasidim*[19] forbids parents from hugging and kissing their children in public, as one must be sensitive to both childless adults, who might see this and long further for the child that they don't have to hug and kiss, and orphaned children, who would long for a parent to hug and kiss them.

The stories of the barrenness of the Matriarchs teach that such circumstances can serve to increase love and sensitivity between husband and wife.[20] The sensitivity is best expressed by Elkanah to his barren wife Hannah, when he told her, "Why are you crying, why won't you eat and why is you heart bitter? Am I not better for you than ten sons?" Perhaps Elkanah meant that he couldn't love Hannah more even if she bore him ten sons. A couple's inability to have children can be cause for them to intensify their love for each other and to consider, if not giving life to an unborn child, then giving hope to a newborn child through adoption.

In his classic work, *The Kuzari*, Rabbi Yehuda HaLevi explains why God appears in the Decalogue as the "God who took you out of Egypt" and not the "God who created heaven and earth." While creation is a much greater event cosmologically, the redemption from Egypt is more meaningful in our relationship.[21] Creation implies a relationship between God and man; redemption proves that the relationship continues and intensifies. If we can compare this to the process of adoption, the ones who raise the child are considered the redeemers and are on a higher level in the relationship than the creators.[22] Rabbinic literature is replete with sources indicating that supporting or teaching a child is tantamount to actually parenting that child.[23]

Midrash Devarim Rabbah refers to a man who has no garment yet makes *tzitzit* (ritual fringes) for others; one who has no house yet makes *mezuzot* for others; one who has no children yet teaches Torah to the children of others. These people will be rewarded, the Midrash says, as if they did the mitzvah themselves. An analysis of this Midrash leads to a startling conclusion. The Midrash refers to a man who can't fulfill the mitzvot of *tzitzit* and *mezuza* yet helps others to do so. He also can't fulfill the obligation of procreating, and yet teaches the children of others Torah! To be consistent, the Midrash should have had him somehow assisting in the process of birth as a doctor or supporter. This source teaches once again that the teaching of Torah to children is in some way a fulfillment of *p'ru ur'vu* (be fruitful and multiply).[24]

In his concluding Messianic prophecies, the prophet Isaiah addresses the strangers and childless, and teaches a powerful message on this topic.

> Thus said the Lord: And let not the eunuch say, "I am a withered tree." For thus said the Lord: "As regards the eunuchs who keep My Sabbaths, who have chosen what I desire and hold

fast to My covenant — I will give them, in My House and within My walls a monument and a name, a *yad vashem*, better than sons and daughters. I will give them an everlasting name which shall not perish.[25]

The childless, Isaiah says, will be given a *yad vashem*,[26] a memorial better than sons and daughters, if they seek justice and specifically observe the Sabbath. The observance of the Sabbath is testimony to God's creation of the world and man.[27] When the Jew observes the Sabbath, he or she is a partner in that creation.[28] Every birth is a Creation, but birth is not the only way we can be party to that first moment of this history of the universe. The observance of Sabbath, the teaching of Torah and the support of a child makes one a party to Creation as well.[29] Once one can come to grips with one's destiny, one can derive and produce the joy and satisfaction that is available to all human beings. One can learn how to intensify the love of one's spouse. One can learn about a whole range of issues that may be plaguing others. And finally, one can come to grips with seeing how one fits in with God's plan, for nothing can change that, and it is always *l'tova*, for the good.

NOTES

1. Niddah 31a.
2. Genesis 1:28 "Be fruitful and multiply."
3. This work, which enumerates the commandments, their laws and reasons, is generally attributed to Rabbi Aaron HaLevi of Barcelona d. circa 1295. See the introduction of Charles Chevelle to the Mossad Harav Kook edition (Jerusalem, 1975), pp. 5-7.
4. *Sefer Hahinukh*, commandment #1, p. 55. Megillah 27a allows for the sale of a Sefer Torah in order to be able to afford to study Torah, and in order to afford to get married. What the study of Torah and marriage have in common is that both provide the opportunity to observe the entire Torah. Hence the statement of the *Sefer Hahinukh*.
5. Taanit 21a.
6. Berachot 5a.
7. Baba Batra 16a.
8. The rabbis and medieval commentaries were not shy to point out the indiscretions and backsliding of the Patriarchs and Matriarchs. See David Berger's on the "Morality of the Patriarchs in Jewish Polemic and Exegesis," reprinted from *Understanding Scripture* (Paulist Press) pp. 49-62, and E. Margaluyot's *HaChayavim B'Mikrah V'Zakaim B'Talmud Uv' Midrashim* (London, 1949) and my M.A. Thesis, "Reflection of Violation of Torah Law in the Bible" Bernard Revel Graduate School, Yeshiva University.
9. See the Rabbis' response to Elisha ben Abuya, Chagigah 14b. See also Ramban, Deuteronomy 1:13. Perhaps Rabbi Akiva's remark to Rabbi Eliezer (Sanhedrin

101a) and Rav Ada's remark to Rav Huna (Berachot 5b) can be explained in this way.
10. Avoda Zara 2b.
11. Sukkah 28b.
12. Ketubot 67b.
13. This is the opinion of Tosafot, Pesachim 28b, s.v. Arel: one does not *require* a medical procedure to determine ability to perform a commandment.
14. See R. Isaac Aremeh's Akedat Yitzhak, beginning of Parashat Toldot, where he expresses the efforts of the Patriarchs and matriarchs in this issue.
15. I Samuel 1:1-2,6,8.
16. Bava Batra 16a; Midrash Hagadol, Genesis 22:1.
17. Pesikta Rabbati: 43
18. Most medieval commentaries consider the 2nd opinion. Rashi, however, maintains the first position. The second opinion expresses its outrage at such behavior and considers the punishment of Penina (losing all ten of her children) as just deserts for such abominable behavior.
19. R. Margaliyot, *Sefer Hasidim*, (Jerusalem, Mossad Harav Kook), pg. 374.
20. Tanna D've Eliyahu: 25 teaches that we should learn from the deeds of the Patriarchs and Matriarchs. In the examples of Abraham and Jacob's insensitivity to Sarah and Rachel's barrenness, we use the Midrash and commentaries to teach what should be derived from their actions. They presumably learned the lesson we have to learn.
21. *Kuzari* 1:87.
22. *Midrash Shemot Rabbah* 46:5 says this explicitly.
23. See especially Sanhedrin 19b where five such cases are enumerated.
24. In fact, it can be shown that the marital act per se is a

fulfillment of *p'ru ur'vu* even if it does not lead to conception. The contention of Tosafot, Chagigah 2b actually refers to the marital act as *p'ru ur'vu*. In fact, the rabbis often referred to the marital act this way. See Berachot 10a. See also R. Shlomo Kluger's Hokhmat Shlomo, Even HaEzer 61:1.
25. Isaiah 56:1-7.
26. The name of the renowned Holocaust memorial in Israel is of course derived from this verse.
27. Exodus 20:8-11.
28. Shabbat 116b.
29. See Malbim, Leviticus 19:2 for an excellent explanation of the juxtaposition of the observance of the Sabbath with commandments regarding parents, both in the Decalogue (Exodus 20:8-12; Deuteronomy 5:12-16) and Leviticus 19:2.

II. Diagnostic Evaluations

INTRODUCTION

Infertility is never a problem that is merely male or merely female. It affects a couple, together, profoundly. Inevitably, however, medical techniques identify the physical source of infertility as residing in one or both of the partners. When the male is involved, special problems arise that pose formidable halakhic challenges.

Within the framework of halakha, it is the man who bears the special commandment to "be fruitful and multiply." (The rabbis explain that women were not specifically commanded to do what already comes naturally to them.) The commandment does not imply, however, free reign to spread one's seed. On the contrary, the halakhic requirement for a man to reproduce comes with an accompanying set of halakhic restrictions on sexual activity that is elaborate in detail. In general, these guidelines serve to strengthen the bonds between husband and wife and to insure the continuity of the Jewish community. Unfortunately, in situations where the cause of infertility resides in the male, those same guidelines may frustrate all attempts at proper diagnosis and treatment.

As a rule, men do not respond as well as women to the need for diagnosic testing, especially physical examinations. Even today, when the value of preventive care has been emphasized, men are more reluctant than women to have annual physical exams. The idea of establishing contact with a physician may be a strange and threatening one, and few regard it as a purely clinical, emotionally neutral exercise. This fear and anxiety which many men feel is understandably compounded for the halakhicly committed man. He may perceive that, should he be found infertile, the solution to his problem will require him to tread on thin halakhic grounds.

These considerations, together with some legitimate halakhic concerns, lead many Orthodox couples to delay the evaluation of the husband entirely until every imaginable test has been performed on the wife. Inevitably, for some couples this only delays proper diagnosis. Still when a male factor is suspected of impeding fertility, it must be properly evaluated.

In the chapter that follows, Dr. Jakobovits outlines the halakhic issues pertinent to the diagnosis of male factor problems. Modern testing of the male is centered mainly around the examination of sperm. It is likely that future tests will also concentrate on methods, albeit more reliable ones, to evaluate sperm. For this reason, the bulk of this chapter is devoted to the issue of sperm procurement for evaluation.

Following this, Dr. Weiss takes up the halakhic

Diagnostic Evaluations 53

issues pertinent to the work-up of the female. Because most of these issues involve the problem of the *niddah* status of the woman, he precedes his discussion with an outline of the basic issues concerning *niddah*.

MALE INFERTILTIY: HALAKHIC ISSUES

Yoel Jakobovits

General Overview of Male Infertility

The perception of the degree of male involvement in infertility has undergone a number of revisions in the past 50 years. Initially, and still in the minds of many, infertility was considered primarily a female problem. As we shall see, however, the halakhic aspects are much more serious in the male than in the female.

The extent of male "liability" is hard to quantify with precision. For example, it is estimated that 40% of infertility is wholly or partly due to male factors.[1] On the other hand, there have been attempts to redefine, in a downward direction, the lower limit of "normal" sperm counts. Thus, many men who previously would have been considered sub-fertile are now considered normal, and the focus has turned back again to the females.[2] Some conditions adversely affecting seminal function include changes in hormone levels, genetic or congenital anatomic abnormalities including retrograde ejaculation, and drug use, toxins, infections, and surgical sequalae; some are discussed below in more detail.

Blood Tests

Subsumed under male infertility are a diagnostically heterogeneous group of disorders. One key basis of discrimination within this group rests upon widely available blood tests. Chief among these are assays of gonadotropins.* A defect in the production of gonadotropins can be measured in the blood by finding low levels of these hormones. Approximately 9% of infertile males belong to this category. Causes include brain tumors and several rare congenital syndromes. Treatment by injections of gonadotropins may be effective in selected cases.

On the other hand, patients with testicular failure will have high levels of circulating gonadotropin hormones.[3] Such patients comprise about 14% of the total number of infertile males. Causes include, in particular, radiotherapy, chemotherapy, and post-infection such as mumps orchitis. Treatment is currently not possible.

By far the largest group of infertile males — 77% — have normal gonadotropin levels. These patients are said to have "post-testicular dysfunction," that is, impairment of the outflow or production of sperm, in spite of normal pituitary and testicular structures. This category encompasses men with mechanically obstructed ejaculatory ducts (6%), infections such as prostatitis and epididymitis which are often transient, varicoceles (37%), and idiopathic (25%).

---

* Gonadotropins are a set of hormones secreted by the pituitary gland in the base of the brain which stimulate (=tropic) the testicular apparatus (=gonads) to produce semen (=sperm and the fluids in which it is suspended).

Varicocele

Celsus, in the first century, described superficial and deep varicoceles and noted the presence of testicular atrophy on the affected side. A varicocele is an abnormal dilation of veins within the spermatic cord. This cord consists of nerves, blood vessels, and spermatic ducts through which the testes are attached to and communicate with the body. These deformities, which probably exert their deleterious effects on sperm production by raising the temperature around the testes,[4] occur on the left side in 90% of cases because of the direct insertion of the spermatic vein into the renal vein on that side. By contrast the right testicular drainage is through the right iliac veins, a venous system with lower resistance pressure. This asymmetric vascular arrangement may also be the basis of the halakhic ruling that injuries to the left testicle (the "weaker one") are less problematic than injuries to the right one, which can be a bar to conjugal union within the genetically Jewish community.[5]

The exact significance of a varicocele — and hence of the indications for surgical obliteration — in the management of infertility is controversial. Approximately 10-15% of males in the general population have a varicocele. There is no evidence that males with normal semen characteristics need corrective treatment even if a varicocele is present.

In men with varicoceles and documented impairment of fertility, surgical correction results in a 30-50% pregnancy rate, although this response rate is very controversial.[6] In spite of lingering questions[7] current practice is to offer correction of varicocele in such men. Surgical interruption of the internal spermatic vein is the usual treatment for clinically apparent varicoceles; there is also a nonsurgical approach that utilizes embolization to occlude the vein.

Halakhically speaking, varicocele repair presents little difficulty. Provided that the medical risks are low and the possibility of fertility improvement are real, one would give every encouragement to correction of this potentially significant impairment.

Sperm evaluation

Most infertility problems, however, are multifactorial in origin — a virtual axiom in all of medicine. Thus varicocele patients often demonstrate specific sperm abnormalities as well, the recognition of which can help in selecting patients for varicocele treatment.[8] The evaluation of sperm characteristics lies at the center of male infertility testing — and at the crux of the halakhic concerns.

Van Leeuwenhoek, the inventor of the microscope, first observed sperm with his new instrument in 1677. However, it was not until 1929 that the modern era of sperm analysis really began.[9] In addition to the initial exclusive emphasis on the sperm itself, attention is now paid to the noncellular biochemical components of the seminal fluid as well.

Semen Procurement

The proper collection of sperm is described in detail in many texts. The following extract from a book[10] on infertility testing is instructive in that it directs us immediately to some of the special problems with which Jewish law is concerned.

> The specimen may be obtained at home or in the physician's office, but it should be kept

warm during transit. It is very unusual for a patient to object to masturbation as a form of inducing ejaculation. When there is an objection, *coitus interruptus* is an alternative method of obtaining the specimen. If the patient has religious objections to both masturbation and withdrawal, he can use a perforated plastic condom manufactured by the Milex Corporation of Chicago, and if he is of the Catholic faith, he may have the condom perforated by a priest. In the rare situation in which none of these methods is satisfactory to the patient, the physician will have to rely on post-coital examination of the ejaculate in the vagina. The patient should understand that an incomplete collection is not only worthless but also misleading.

Halakhic misgivings are prompted by every option summarized in this excerpt. The collection of sperm, masturbation, *coitus interruptus*, and the use of condoms — they are all of concern to the halakha. Notwithstanding the strongly pro-procreative attitudes outlined earlier, there are several halakhic principles which pull in the antithetical direction, curtailing any routine or automatic authorization to investigate male infertility.

By omitting explicit condemnation of masturbation, the Torah[11] has promoted much discussion as to the precise categorization of this prohibition. The "improper emission of genital seed"[12] is regarded as fitting within the general heading of prohibited sexual relations by some,[13] as a "free-standing" prohibition by others,[14] or as merely of rabbinic origin by yet others.[15] In addition to these negative aspects, improper emission of seed may be forbidden as a breach of the obligation to have children.[16] However, another authority[17] holds that the ban on conscious wastage of seed is entirely unrelated to the mitzvah of procreation. Other candidates for the classification into which masturbation fits are the interdictions forbidding wastage in general,[18] and censuring eroticism even when only by contemplation,[19] let alone by performance.

The Torah records its condemnation of the wastefulness of seed in two historical settings. It was the sin which is thought by many commentaries to have been a principal reason for the Flood in Noah's days.[20] Secondly, it was the transgression of Er and Onan,[21] an occurrence which gave rise to the term "onanism." Chief among the several sinful ingredients in Onan's act is its association with *coitus interruptus*, a topic which prompts apparently contradictory views in the Talmudic literature.

Despite the Onan story, with its unequivocal censuring tones, there is a Talmudic[22] record of R. Eliezer's opinion who actually recommended the practice of *coitus interruptus*! He taught so in order to protect a lactating mother from a second pregnancy which could endanger the existing infant by diminishing the mother's milk supply. Rabbi Moshe Feinstein, the recently-deceased, universally acknowledged premier halakhic adjudicator, comments: "Since this is the same R. Eliezer in whose name the Talmud quotes a dictum warning against even unintentional improper emission of seed, his endorsement of *coitus interruptus* for reasons of the health of the child is all the more instructive. It means that, to him at least, seed is not said to be "uselessly" destroyed if a proper purpose is served thereby, and if this is the only manner in which that purpose can now be served. Marital relations is that purpose: since normal intercourse would cause a hazard to health, the emission of seed for such relations, where there is no alternative, is not wasteful; where there is an alternative it is, even according to him."[23]

The normative ruling, however, is in accordance with the Sages' dissenting opinion. Ergo Maimonides prohibits the practice without equivocation: "It is forbidden to destroy seed. Therefore, a man may not practice *coitus interruptus*, etc."[24]

The strict attitudes regarding *coitus interruptus*[25] should be considered alongside, and in contrast with, the somewhat more lenient attitudes towards "unnatural intercourse (*bi'ah she-lo k'darkah*)." The prevailing Talmudic view is that "a man may do with his wife as he wishes."[26] Tosafot[27] records two notable formulae proposed by R. Yitzhak to resolve the law's permissiveness in Nedarim as compared with the restrictive attitude held in Yevamot. Firstly, the tolerant view sanctioning unnatural intercourse may have assumed that no semination occurs. Alternatively, semination is in fact tolerated provided unnatural intercourse is resorted to only on occasion and that the contraceptive intention of the husband is not constant.

This second answer of R. Yitzhak — highlighting both "intent" and "irregularity" — may constitute broad foundation for authorization to practice unnatural intercourse within marriage when it fulfills a "purpose." Even the assuagement of the husband's sexual desire may be included within the parameters of acceptable standards of sexual relations, this being reaffirmed by many authorities.[28] All authorities emphasize, however, that this general license is controversial and certainly applies only to occasional sexual expression.[29]

There are several instances where prominent early sources sanctioned masturbation — and the inevitable spillage of seed to which it leads — to achieve an overriding "purpose." A man may resort to masturbation in order to relieve an otherwise uncontrollable sexual desire, thereby avoiding an even graver transgression of a prohibited sexual relationship.[30] The Talmud[31] itself recommended masturbation for the investigation of sexual impotence (erectile dysfunction), a disability which can preclude marriage within the genetically Jewish community. Some authorities[32] also sanctioned masturbation in order to ascertain whether post-coital vaginal bleeding derives from the male or from the female. Post-coital bleeding in the female may pose restrictions on the resumption of sexual relations.

Other specific "purposes" may also be acceptable reasons to sanction a lenient attitude. Medical[33] considerations — though not specified — would be generally pardoned and can provide halakhic grounds for sanctioning this method for temporary birth control. This is clearly articulated by Rabbi Isaiah da Trani[34] who writes: "...how [in the light of the sin of Er and Onan] did the Sages permit unnatural intercourse [as when using a diaphragm[35]] when it involves [wasteful] emission of seed? The answer is: Wherever the husband's intent is to avoid pregnancy so as not to mar his wife's beauty and he does not want to fulfill the mitzvah of procreation, it is forbidden. But if his intent is to spare her physical

Diagnostic Evaluations   63

hazard, then it is permitted. So also if he does so for his own pleasure [unnatural intercourse is permitted]...for 'a man may do with his wife what he wishes.'" Strikingly, as Feldman[36] points out, though this passage was written in the thirteenth century but remained unpublished until 1931, it nevertheless reflects an oft-repeated mainstream opinion. It has been used to provide significant support for lenient rulings by several twentieth century halakhic masters such as the late Chief Rabbi of Israel, Rabbi Isaac Herzog,[37] and Rabbi Moshe Feinstein.[38]

It should be noted, however, that there is a notable body of extra-halakhic Cabalistic literature[39] which inveighs heavily against any spillage of seed under any circumstance. Reflecting this view is the comment[40] of Rav Yosef Karo: "Had R. Yitzhak seen what the Zohar says about the gravity of *hash-hatat zera*, namely that it is the most severe of sins, he never would have written what he did." Both the permissive and restrictive opinions are recorded by Rabbi Moshe Isserles.[41]

These considerations form the foundation upon which the halakhic position regarding masturbation is based. Of paramount importance is purpose. When the intention is procreation, either directly (through artificial insemination and in vitro fertilization) or indirectly (when evaluating male infertility), there is significant room for leniency within the halakhic guidelines.

It is important to recognize that no *carte blanche* regarding the method of semen procurement, even under conditions of need and sanction, is granted. Justification for a tolerant approach exists only in special circumstances, as in the investigation of male infertility. For example, by recommending either warm perianal applications (Rava) or visually evocative stimuli (Abaye) to arouse ejaculation, the Talmud[42] itself appears to be deliberately avoiding any suggestion of direct penile stimulation to avoid conflict with the Talmud's (Niddah 13a) express admonition against such contact. A similar reluctance may have prompted the "teach us, our Rabbi" phrase used to establish an acceptable method of penile evaluation. The expression assumes that there is difficulty with the seemingly obvious technique, masturbation.[43]

Specifically germane to our discussion here are the expressed rabbinic positions regarding procurement of sperm by masturbation in the medical investigation of male infertility.[44] Mindful of the pro-procreative intent of the procedure, where no other technique is appropriate, some[45] authorities sanction such artificial collection of sperm. Others[46] however, disagree, arguing that because of the many technical uncertainties[47] coupled with the strongly condemnatory Talmudic and, in particular, Cabalistic pronouncements, masturbation can never be sanctioned — even in the interest of siring offspring. Similarly, some[48] even have argued that because of the severity of the sin of masturbation, one would rather recommend that a childless couple divorce and remarry someone else! Mindful of the limited likelihood of helpful medical intervention, several authorities[49] are similarly disinclined to sanction masturbation even with the intention of aiding procreation.

On the other hand, more lenient views exist as well. Chief among these opinions are the previously quoted views of Rabbi Yaakov Emden and Rabbi Chaim O. Grodzinski. The latter suggests that, if possible, it is better to collect seminal fluid from a condom[50] worn during intercourse, thereby avoiding masturbation. More contemporaneous decisors[51] have also suggested this method as most acceptable. In addition, Beit Shmuel,[52] citing the same Talmudic passages, also deduces a liberal attitude with respect to semen procurement in pressing circumstances. Accordingly, where post-coital bleeding is detected, he permits the non-coital ejaculation of sperm to establish whether hematospermia is responsible. This license may only be appropriate when the evaluation of the female companion is not conclusive.[53]

A leading contemporary halakhist, Rabbi S. Z. Auerbach[54], has ruled that "even when he has a male and a female child [the halakhic minimum] a man is permitted to obtain sperm [notwithstanding the severe restrictions which would normally apply] in order to fulfill the imperative of *la-shevet* [see earlier discussion, page 6] or where his wife is in significant [psychological] distress in not having more children." However, the precise method of procuring sperm is not indicated.

Yet another approach might be applied in situations of infertile couples where investigations already undertaken fail to identify any female disorder. Here it may be fair to assume that the male either has no viable sperm or has defective sperm. In either case, wastage of his seed would not constitute *zera l'vatalah*, there being no likely viable seed to speak of. This line of reasoning is developed by Rabbi S. B. Sofer[55] who concludes by advising that "where it is possible, a post-coital diaphragm may be used; even during coitus one may be lenient for this purpose.... But if it is impossible [to use the semen collected] by a diaphragm, then my opinion is to be lenient [about manual masturbation]....However, since I failed to find absolute proof, and due to the gravity of the issue, I would solicit additional [concurring] opinions...."

Summary of Semen Collection Methods

The reader may be excused if he is left quite bewildered by the foregoing account of widely differing views. A workable algorithm of graduated choices along the lines of Rabbi E. Waldenberg's[56] is suggested:

— The preferred method of semen collection is from the vagina following normal coitus.[57]

— Where that is not possible because of technical or emotional reasons, sperm may be procured after *coitus interruptus*.[58]

— Where that is unsuitable, the collection should be made using a condom, preferably one with a perforation, worn during intercourse.[59]

— If that is impossible a collecting receptacle should be placed intravaginally.

— Finally, if that too is impractical, sperm may be obtained by masturbation. Penile stimulation should preferably be achieved by a mechanical stimulator, though self-stimulation is also permitted.[60]

Testicular Biopsy

Occasionally, biopsy of the testicle is indispensable to accurate diagnosis. It is usually recommended in azoospermic men with normal-sized testes to discriminate between ductal obstruction and spermatogenic failure. In men with poor quality sperm or very low counts, results of histological evaluation will rarely, if ever, alter therapy. The biopsy will assist, however, in making a definitive diagnosis which can aid the physician in providing the patient with a reliable prognosis, thereby avoiding needless treatment in unsalvageable circumstances.

Evidently, the futility of testicular biopsy was assumed by one early halakhic writer[61] who reports that "none of the physicians of my town are familiar with such a test". Nevertheless, he proceeds to discuss the halakhic concerns in some detail. The obstacles relate in particular to the Biblical injunction proscribing marital bonds with a genetically Jewish woman by any man who has "wounded testes or severed membrum."[62] The Talmud[63] elaborates this injunction to include any wounding or crushing injury to the penis, testes or cords of the testes. The author concludes that testicular biopsy would be permitted from a "wounded or crushed" point of view in that the perforation in the testes heals completely. However, he regards this method of semen procurement as "unnatural" emission of seed and therefore rules against it. He does not speak of actual biopsy of the testicle.

Arguments[64] allowing the procedure because testicular sperm are immature prior to their maturation in the collecting ducts and therefore would not be subject to any restrictions on sperm emission have been advanced. Furthermore, the prohibition on surgical damage to the genitalia might be applicable only where the patient has reproductive capacity, a precondition clearly not extant in the investigation of an infertile male.[65] Similarly, Rabbi Feinstein[66] also sanctions testicular biopsy, arguing that the Talmudic constraints are applicable only when the perforation of the testis results in infertility; nowadays the procedure has the reverse likelihood, being designed to help alleviate infertility.

NOTES

1. R.F. Blackwell and M.P. Steinkampf, "Infertility: Diagnosis and Therapy," In *Controversies in Reproductive Endocrinology and Infertility*, ed. M.R. Soules (N.Y.: Elsevier, 1989), p. 15.
2. C.M.K. Nelson and R.G. Bunge, "Semen Analysis: Evidence for Changing Parameters of Male Fertility Potential," *Fertil Steril* 25:503 (1974).
3. Because the pituitary gland tries to drive the unresponsive testes, unrestricted by the negative biofeedback which successful spermatogenesis would provide.
4. Alternative suggestions — none of which have been adequately substantiated — include different concentrations of adrenal hormone exposure to the testes and decreased testicular blood flow. E. Steinberg, "Male Infertility," in *Gynecologic Endocrinology*, ed. J.J. Gold and J.B. Josimovich, 4th edition (1987); pp. 572-3.
5. See fuller discussion below, in section 6 regarding testicular biopsies.
6. A.T.K. Crockett, H Takihara and M.J. Cosentino, "The Varicocele," *Fertil Steril* 41:5 (1984).
7. A. Vermeulen and M. Vandeweghe, "Improved Fertility After Varicocele Correction: Fact or Fiction?" *Fertil Steril* 42:249 (1984).
8. B.J. Rogers, G.G. Mygatt, D.W. Soderdahl and R.W.

Hale, "Monitoring of Suspected Infertile Men With Varicocele by the Sperm Penetration Assay," *Fertil Steril* 44:800 (1985).
9. D. Macomber and M.B. Sanders, "The Spermatozoa Count," *N Engl J Med* 200:981 (1929). An up-to-date discussion is provided by B.C. Dunphy, L.M. Neal and I.D. Cooke, "The Clinical Value of Conventional Semen Analysis," *Fertil Steril* 51:324 (1989).
10. R.J. Sherins and S.S. Howards, "Male Infertility," in *Campbell's Urology*, ed. P.C. Walsh, 5th edition (Philadelphia: W.B. Saunders, 1986), p. 645.
11. The primary Talmudic source is in Niddah 13a (see Magid Mishna, Yad HaHazaka, Issurei Bi'ah 21:18).
12. Known in Hebrew as either *hotza'at zera l'vatalah* or more commonly as *hash-hatat zera*, generally regarded as interchangeable phrases. Feldman, *Marital Relations*, p. 109, cites *Resp. Hinukh Beit Yitzhak*, Even HaEzer, no. 7, who proposes a plausible distinction between the two.
13. Rambam, Yad HaHazaka, Issurei Bi'ah 21:18, Tur Shulhan Arukh, Even HaEzer 23:1 based on Exodus 20:13. Cf. Rambam's Mishnah Commentary, Sanhedrin 54a.
14. Semak, no. 292; Ma'adanei Yom Tov on Rosh, Niddah 2:40. Contemporary discussions: Rabbi M. Feinstein, Resp. Iggrot Moshe, Even HaEzer 3:14 staunchly reiterates the biblical nature of this transgression; Rabbi E. Waldenberg, Resp. Tzitz Eliezer IX, 51:1.1 cites various opinions but comes to no firm conclusion.
15. Resp. P'nei Yehoshua, Even HaEzer II, no. 44.2. argues that the severe strictures applied by the Sages are exaggerated and were meant to underscore the repulsiveness with which they regarded onanism.

An unusual analysis is suggested by Hagga'ot Ezer

Mikodesh cited by R. A.M. Babad, Resp. Imrei Tova, no. 33: "The [Biblical] prohibition of wasteful spillage of seed pertains only prior to the ban on polygamy promulgated by Rabbeinu Gershom ben Yehuda (c. 1000) when [by having several wives] it may have been possible for *each* ejaculation to achieve fruition. Today — especially in our countries where secular laws makes [even] divorce difficult — the matter has changed and the halakha has changed and there is no more than a rabbinic prohibition here." R. Babad also quotes his uncle, the author of Resp. Havatzelet Hasharon (Addenda to Even HaEzer. vol. 1), who concluded similarly that today spillage of seed is only a rabbinic prohibition. I am grateful to my brother-in-law, Rabbi C.Z. Pearlman of London, for directing me to these citations.

16. Tosafot, Sanhedrin 59b. Those excluded from the mitzvah of procreation would therefore be free from this restriction (Rabbeinu Tam, Tosafot, Yevamot 12b, s.v. *shalosh*).
17. Ramban, Niddah 13a.
18. "*Bal tashchit*" (Deuteronomy 20:19), undoubtedly civilization's earliest conservation legislation! Rabbi Yaakov Ettlinger, Resp. Binyan Tzion, No.137 and novellae Arukh L'Ner, Niddah 13b makes this tentative suggestion. He also suggests that this interdiction may be based upon a *halakha l'Moshe m-Sinai*.
19. See Ahiezer III, 24:5 based on Deuteronomy 23:10 and Avoda Zara 20b.
20. Genesis 6:12; alluded to by Rashi, 6:11. See also Avot D'Rav Nassan 32:1; Zohar I, 66:2 on Genesis 7:4; Ramban and Ritvah on Niddah 13a; Rabbi Menachem M. Kasher, in Torah Shleimah, Genesis 6:12, in note to no. 150, comparing similar suggestions in Shabbat 41a.

21. Genesis 38:7-10 and the Talmud's discussion thereof, in Yevamot 34b. The passage in Yevamot equates the sin of Er and Onan with unnatural intercourse (*shelo k'darkah*) rather than with Rashi's assumption (on Genesis, loc. cit.) that the failing was *coitus interruptus*. See Ritvah and Maharsha, on Yevamot 34b and Ibn Ezra, on Genesis 38:7 who offer a variety of approaches to reconcile these differing interpretations. See the trenchant passage in Levush, Genesis 38:10.
22. R. Eliezer, on Yevamot 34b, a position with which the Hakhamim — the Sages — disagree.
23. Resp. Iggrot Moshe, Even HaEzer 1:63 as translated by Feldman, *Marital Relations,* p.152.
24. Yad HaHazaka, Hilkhot Issurie Bi'ah 21:18; Semag, neg. 126; Shulhan Arukh, Even HaEzer 23:1.
25. Not all authorities are always strict; some advocate *coitus interruptus* as the desirable method to obtain sperm for analysis: Resp. Z'kan Aaron 1:66, 67 and 2:96, p.18 no. 67.
26. Nedarim 20b. See Beit Yosef on Tur, Even HaEzer 25; Kol Bo, Hilkhot Ishut, p. 66a paragraph 76 who counsel caution to the pious.
27. Yevamot 34b, s.v. *v'lo*.
28. Tur, Even HaEzer 25 and Orah Haim 240; Yam Shel Shlomo, Yevamot, 3:18, and Hagga'ot HaBah on Rosh (Yevamot 34b) and others refer to a permissive ruling by Rosh, Yevamot, 3:6 — a text absent (deleted?) in extant versions of this commentary. Similarly Drisha on Tur, Even HaEzer 23:1; Resp. Maishiv Davar, Yoreh De'ah 88; Resp. Iggrot Moshe, Even HaEzer 1:63, who also records his pleasure to hear that Resp. Tzemah Tzedek, Even Haezer 89 supported this position.

29. For example, Rama, Even HaEzer 25:2: "A man may act with his wife as he wishes, having intercourse when he wants...[and how he wants] provided he does not ejaculate. Others are lenient and rule that he may have unnatural intercourse even if he emits sperm so long as this is not habitual. However even though all this is [strictly speaking] permitted, 'He who sanctifies himself [by denying even] that which is permitted is called holy.'"
30. R. Yehuda HaHasid, Sefer Hassidim, No: 176; but Hiddah (Petah Einayim, Niddah 13) dismisses this as a case of unavoidable spillage and not of intentional masturbation.
31. Yevamot 76a.
32. Beit Shmuel, Even HaEzer 25:2.
33. Levush, Even HaEzer 23:5, though dyspareunia — painful intercourse — may not be an acceptable reason to suspend the restrictions (Resp. Melamed Lehoil III, 18).
34. Tosafot RiD (R. Yeshiyah D'Atun), Yevamot 12b.
35. Although the expression 'unnatural' intercourse customarily denotes non-vaginal (e.g. anal or oral) sex, any form of frustrated or aberrant vaginal (e.g. by a diaphragm or other intra-vaginal device) penetration may be subsumed under this label.
36. Feldman, *Marital Relations*, p. 162
37. Resp. Heikhal Yitzhak, Even HaEzer 2:16.
38. Resp. Iggrot Moshe, Even HaEzer 63, 64.
39. In particular the Zohar II 259a and 263b. Similarly strongly worded restrictive views are recorded by Sefer Haredim III, ch. 2 by R. Eliezer Azikri (1601) and in R. Isaiah Hurvitz's Shnei Luhot HaBrit (Sh'lah) I, Sha'ar HaOtiot 100a, b. The latter, on p. 102b (Amsterdam ed.) writes: "Study to observe all the laws of marital

relations as enumerated in the Tur, Orach Chaim 240 and Even HaEzer 25. Omit nothing ...A man should know every word by heart — except in the matter of unnatural intercourse. In that connection I have cited (the restrictive) words of Sefer Haredim — to him you should listen [rather than to the Tur]."

40. Rabbi Y. Karo, Bedek Habayit on Beit Yosef, Even HaEzer 25.
41. Shulhan Arukh, Even HaEzer 25:2.
42. Normally, men with rabbinically-identified anatomical disfigurement of the penis are barred from wedding a genetically Jewish spouse; undamaged anatomy and function of sexual organs are prerequisites for such relationships. Elaborating, the Talmud (Yevamot 76a) states: "If a hole which had been made in the [penile] corona itself is closed, the man is disqualified if it reopens when semen is emitted; but if it does not [reopen the man is deemed] fit. Rava the son of Rabbah sent to R. Joseph: Will our Master instruct us how to proceed [with a test when it is desired to ascertain whether the semen will reopen an occluded perforation]? The other replied: Warm barley bread is procured, and placed upon the man's anus. This stimulates the flow of semen and the effect can be observed. Said Abaye: Is everybody like our father Jacob...because [of whose saintliness] he never before [marriage] experienced the emission of semen? [An alternative technique was offered by] Abaye who said: No, colored [female] garments are dangled before him. Said Rava: Is everybody then like Barzillai the Gileadite [known for his indulgences]? In fact it is obvious that the original answer is to be maintained."
43. R. Shlomo Luria, Yam Shel Shlomo, Yevamot 8:16.
44. Quite another application of the restriction of mastur-

bation is found in the laws of circumcision. A tense penis is recommended prior to the procedure to assure safe amputation of the foreskin and thus reduce the risk of injury to the underlying glands. This is especially true in the adult. It is permissible for erection to be achieved by physical stimulation of the penis but since this can lead to *hotza'at zera l'vatalah* it ought to have been banned because of the Talmud's opposition to manual masturbation as recorded in Niddah 13a. Rabbi Shlomo Kluger (introduction to *Sefer Kin'at Sofrim*) eliminates this apparent difficulty: in accordance with the general rule that positive commandments take precedence over negative ones, especially when the former are Biblical and the latter rabbinic in origin, circumcision takes precedence over the ordinance banning masturbation. Based upon these considerations it is arguable that in spite of whatever rabbinic restrictions may exist, masturbation would still be permitted when it is performed to facilitate reproductive capability. However, a counter-argument might point out that in the case of circumcision seminal spillage is not inevitable; in the case of infertility it is.

45. Rabbi C. O. Grodzinski, Ahiezer III, 24:4 partly based upon Rabbi Yaakov Emden, Resp. She'elat Ya'avetz I, 43; Rabbi Uziel, Resp. Mishpetei Uziel, Even HaEzer 42. Resp. Z'kan Aaron I:67 insists upon coitus interruptus rather than masturbation.

    Semen analysis and procurement are discussed in detail by many authorities including: Rabbi E. Waldenberg, Resp. Tzitz Eliezer VII, 48:1.7 and IX, 51:1; Rabbi O. Yosef, Resp. Yabia Omer II, Even HaEzer 1:7 and Rabbi M. Feinstein, Resp. Iggrot Moshe vol. 3, Even HaEzer 1:70, Even HaEzer 2:16,

Even HaEzer 3:14, and Even HaEzer 4:27.
A valuable review of semen destruction and contraception in general appears in the *Reb Yaakov Rosenheim Jubilee Volume*, (New York, 1932), p. 87 by Rabbi J. Z. Horowitz of Frankfurt. He gathers the major opinions and concludes that seminal procurement for analysis intended to facilitate procreation is permissible.

46. Otzar HaPoskim, Even HaEzer, IX, p. 86a (quoting in particular Resp. Divrei Malkiel 5:157; Vaya'an Avraham, no. 7; R.S. Engel (quoted below), etc.

47. Uncertainties include: The impediment may be in the female partner; there may in any case be no effective therapy; it may be possible for him to father children were he married to someone else; a problem with the technique of intercourse may exist.

48. In his Responsa (6:75) Rabbi S. Engel recommends this radical answer after ten years of barren marriage have transpired. See S. Shilo, "Impotence as a Ground for Divorce (To the End of the Period of the Rishonim)," *The Jewish Law Annual* 4:127-43 (1981) for an interesting historical review.

49. Hayyim Hezekiah Medini, Sedei Hemed, "Ma'arekhet Ishut," sec.13, in the Pe'at Sadeh supplement, Rabbi A.Y. Kook's Resp. Ezrat Kohen, Hilknot Ishut, no. 32; Resp. Avnei Nezer, Even HaEzer 83. They advocate empiric therapeutic trials without regard to specific diagnoses. On the other hand, Resp. Tzitz Eliezer IX, 51:1.2 acknowledges that modern differential diagnoses may indeed have a significant impact on treatment choices. Rabbi Eliezer of Munkacz, author of Resp. Minhat Eliezer, in Darkhei Teshuva, Hilkhot Niddah agrees with the restrictive views but would sanction the post-coital vaginal collection of sperm for analysis.

50. Rabbis Y. Neuwirth and S. Z. Auerbach are quoted by A. Abraham in Nishmat Avraham, Even HaEzer 23:2, p. 112 as recommending that when a condom is worn a small perforation should be made, thus enabling sperm to enter the female's reproductive tracts. This would obviate concerns about wastefulness of seed in that it is possible that the coital act will result in pregnancy.

    Of tangential interest here — but of potentially wider application in situations of barrier prevention of sexually transmitted diseases — is a recently published responsum by R. Waldenberg (Resp. Tzitz Eliezer, XX, 50) permitting the use of a condom for a "temporary period" by a male whose partner develops intense post-coital vaginitis. R. Waldenberg cites R. Naftali T. Y. Berlin (Resp. Mayshiv Davar, Yoreh De'ah, 88) who rules leniently when the purpose of condom use is prompted by the wife's health rather than *hashchatat zera* per se. Similarly, he cites the original analysis of the Goan of Rogachov (Resp. Tzaphnat Paneach, 164) permitting a tightly placed condom, since sperm cannot be ejaculated, for so long as the ejaculate does not exit it does not acquire the status of zera with respect to halakhic restrictions. When I asked R. Waldenberg how to advise a couple where the man has AIDS, he suggested the use of a condom for a "temporary period" of about a year. The question was to be revisited again, as no blanket license was given.
51. Rabbi Y.Y. Weis, Resp. Minhat Yitzhak 3:108.6.
52. Shulhan Arukh, Even HaEzer 25:2.
53. Rabbi Waldenberg, Resp. Tzitz Eliezer, *loc cit,* takes issue with the opinion of Mahatzit Hashekel, cited by Beit Shmuel, Even HaEzer 25:2 *loc cit,* who maintains that the dispensation of *hotza'at shikhvat zera l'vatalah*

implied by Yvamot 76a is limited to when the investigation is needed to establish marriageability within the genetically Jewish community, R. Waldenberg argues that avoiding divorce is no less a reason for permissiveness. Evidence of spermatogenesis may be required to overcome restrictions which pertain to certain categories of infertile men. Such investigations, of course, must be made on the male in question. Rabbi Waldenberg cites Taharat Yisrael, Orah Haim 240:39 who rules that ejaculation is permitted when physicians are undertaking investigations designed to promote fertility and eventual procreation.

54. Quoted by A. Avraham in Nishmat Avraham, Even HaEzer 23:2, p. 111. By contrast, R. Eliyahu Bakshi-Doron of Haifa (Binyan Av II and cited in a personal communication to Dr. Joel B. Wolowelsky, Ph.D., dated December 15, 1991) submits that the grave ban on *hotza'at zera* could not be lifted for purposes other than the mitzvah of *p'ru ur'vu*. The rabbinically invoked mitzvah of *la-shevet* would not in itself authorize annulment of this *issur*.

55. Resp. Shevet Sofer, Even HaEzer 1. Similar arguments are found in Resp. Imrei Esh, Yoreh De'ah 69 and Resp. Levushei Mordekhai III, Orah Haim 51. A contrasting view is that of Resp. Rav Pealim III, Even HaEzer 2.

56. Resp. Tzitz Eliezer, *loc. cit*, end of "Gate" 1.

57. A. Avraham in Nishmat Avraham, Even HaEzer 23:2, p. 112 reports that Rabbi S.Z. Auerbach recommends that if possible this be performed by a female doctor or nurse.

58. As recommended by Resp. Z'kan A'aron 1:66; but see next note.

59. Though other authorities would reverse this step with

the previous one.
60. In accordance with Resp. Ahiezer, but in contrast with Resp. Iggrot Moshe which would never allow self-stimulation.
61. Resp. Z'kan A'aron 1:66. He assumed the purpose of this test to be the analysis of the semen.
62. Devarim 23:2.
63. Yevamot 75b.
64. Rabbi Y. Neuwirth quoted by A. Avraham in Nishmat Avraham, Even HaEzer 23:2, p. 113.
65. Rabbi Y.Y. Weis, Resp. Minhat Yitzhak 3:108.7. In view of Rabbeinu Tam's opinion which permits even complete excision of the left testicle, Rabbi Weis counsels that an elective biopsy be taken from the left side. Rabbi E. Waldenberg, Resp. Tzitz Eliezer IX, 51:1.2 agrees with him.
66. Resp. Iggrot Moshe, Even HaEzer 2:3:2. Note that Rabbi Feinstein does not make his authorization contingent upon using the left side only. See also J.A. Gordon, R.D. Amelar, L. Dubin and M.D. Tendler, "Infertility Practice and Orthodox Jewish Law," *Fertil Steril* 28:480, (1975).

DIAGNOSTIC PROCEDURES IN THE FEMALE PATIENT

Richard Weiss

INTRODUCTION TO THE LAWS OF *NIDDAH*

The halakhot (religious laws) surrounding a woman's menstrual cycle form the basic backdrop of our discussion as they govern the normal sexual life of a religiously committed Jewish couple. An understanding of these basic concepts is indispensable to the professional managing fertility therapy for an observant couple.

In general, this is a very complicated area of halakha and requires a particular expertise to be able to render proper judgments. There is a core of Biblical law surrounded by a host of rabbinic legislation. On a practical level, individuals do not differentiate between Biblical and rabbinic prohibitions. However, when a rabbi is faced with a difficult set of social circumstances, the fact that a particular prohibition might be rabbinic rather than Biblical gives him legitimate leeway in addressing the problem.

Biblically, there is a distinction between a *niddah*, a woman who experiences vaginal bleeding derived from the uterus during her expected menstrual period, and a *zavah*, a woman who experiences bleeding at times other than during her expected period.[1] The definitions include other factors as well, but the presentation here is aimed at providing a basic background for the chapter. A woman is a *niddah* for seven days from the onset of bleeding, regardless of whether the flow is continuous, assuming that the bleeding has stopped prior to sunset of the seventh day.[2] At the end of the seventh day, the woman performs an internal examination to be certain that the bleeding has actually stopped.[3] A *zavah* begins a sequence of seven clean days only after all bleeding has ceased, at which time she too performs an internal examination to ascertain this fact.[4] Both women immerse themselves in a *mikveh* (ritualarium) after the conclusion of the seventh day.[5] From the onset of bleeding until the conclusion of the seven days, all sexual intercourse and other physical modes of affection are prohibited between the woman and her husband.[6] It is only after immersion in the *mikveh* that these restrictions are lifted.[7]

Biblically, an important condition necessary for a woman to become either a *niddah* or a *zavah* is that of sensation.[8] Three major views exist as to what constitutes an appropriate sensation.[9] They are: a kind of tremor or shaking of the body, a sensation of something detaching from the uterine wall, or the sensation of something flowing internally similar to the sensation of urination. We will return to the issue of sensation later in the discussion.

The laws of *niddah* have developed through various stages. As the law was accepted in the time of the Talmud, the distinction between a *niddah* and a *zavah* became less relevant.[10] In practice, any minute amount of bleeding — with or without any associated sensation and regardless of the timing of such bleeding — invokes the stringencies of both a *niddah* and a *zavah*.[11] In addition, all bleeding must cease before observing a required interval of seven clean days.[12] The woman goes to the *mikveh* on the evening following the conclusion of the seventh clean day (days begin and end at sunset, not sunrise) and is then permitted to have intimate relations with her husband.[13] This halakha applies to spotting as well.[14] Furthermore, any amount of bleeding or spotting during the seven clean days cancels this sequence retroactively, thus requiring a new seven-day series.[15]

The Rama, Rabbi Moses Isserles (c.1520-1572) quotes the additional accepted practice that a woman does not begin the seven day sequence until at least five days after the onset of menstrual bleeding or spotting.[16] The first day of bleeding is included in these five additional days.[17] (The reason for this rabbinical amendment is related in some way to the impurity that the semen deposited in the woman's reproductive tract can cause.[18] The halakha, however, applies regardless of any actual intercourse having taken place.[19]) Thus a woman committed to following the halakha is unable to have sexual relations with her husband for a minimum of twelve days, regardless of the length of her menstrual bleeding or spotting. For example, if a woman's first day of menstruation occurs between Saturday night and Sunday evening, she must wait until Thursday when, if the flow has ceased, she performs an internal examination before sunset to verify this fact and begins the seven day sequence that night. During the seven days, she must continue to perform internal examinations with a cloth or pad.[20] (The details of the method of examination, the nature of the cloth used and frequency of exams are beyond the scope of this introduction. Rabbi Shimon Eider's *Halachos of Niddah* provides an excellent review of these details. It is important to stress, however, that in any practical situation a competent rabbi should be consulted.) Assuming that no further bleeding occurred during the seven clean days, the sequence ends on the following Thursday evening, at which time she immerses herself in a *mikveh*.

In the course of our discussion, we will mention the positions of classic and contemporary rabbinic authorities whose opinions have wide currency in the halakhic community. While the names may be irrelevant for the medical professional, they are important for the rabbinic authorities who address these issues. (Dates are not given for contemporary authorities.)

BASIC PRINCIPLES
A. Anatomy
The diagnostic procedures used in the evaluation of the infertile woman touch upon four major issues within the laws of *niddah*. The first one is that of anatomy. We begin, therefore, with a brief description of the female reproductive tract.[21]

The female anatomy is divided into "external" and "internal" organs. The external organs include the labia majora and minora, clitoris, vestibule, urethral opening and hymen. The labia (lips) majora are two rounded folds of adipose tissue, or fat, covered with skin and hair. They cover the labia minora, which are two flat folds of skin which are reddish in color. The labia minora converge superiorly, or above, to form the clitoris, a small cylinder-like body similar in some respects to the male penis. The area enclosed by the labia minora is termed the vestibule. The urethra (from the urinary bladder) opens into the vestibule as does the vagina. The vagina opens into the lower portion of the vestibule and the urethra above that. The hymen is a skin like membrane, or covering, that surrounds the vaginal opening more or less completely. It has a small opening which allows for blood to flow out. Because it contains many blood vessels, tearing of the hymen during the first intercourse usually results in bleeding. On occasion, the hymen is resistant to penetration by the penis and a surgical procedure is required to open it.

The vagina, the first of the internal organs, is an elastic, muscular tube that extends to the uterus. It sits between the urinary bladder anteriorly (toward the front of the body) and rectum posteriorly (toward the back of the body). It functions in intercourse and as the birth canal. The cervix, or neck of the uterus, projects into the upper end of the vagina. The cervix is positioned in relation to the vagina at a 45°-90° angle. It has two oses, or openings: the external os (mouth) that opens into the vagina and the internal os that opens into the uterus. They are separated by the cervical canal, which measures about three to four centimeters in length. The external os is usually open about three millimeters in diameter (Figure 1).

The uterus is a flattened, pear shaped, muscular organ lined with a tissue called the endometrium. It, too, sits between the bladder and rectum and is continuous with the cervix below. The Fallopian tubes are connected to the uterus. At their other ends, they lie in close proximity to the ovaries. Sperm are transmitted to this region of the tube via the vagina, cervix and uterus. Mature eggs are captured in this area of the tube during the process of ovulation, which is the release of an egg directly through the surface of the ovary. If the egg is fertilized, the resulting embryo is then propelled toward the uterus, where it implants and develops into an embryo and fetus.

The menstrual cycle is a series of regular cyclic changes that occur in preparation for pregnancy. If implantation does not take place, the endometrium is shed. This spontaneous shedding is associated with bleeding, primarily from arteries supplying the uterine lining. The menstrual flow contains dead

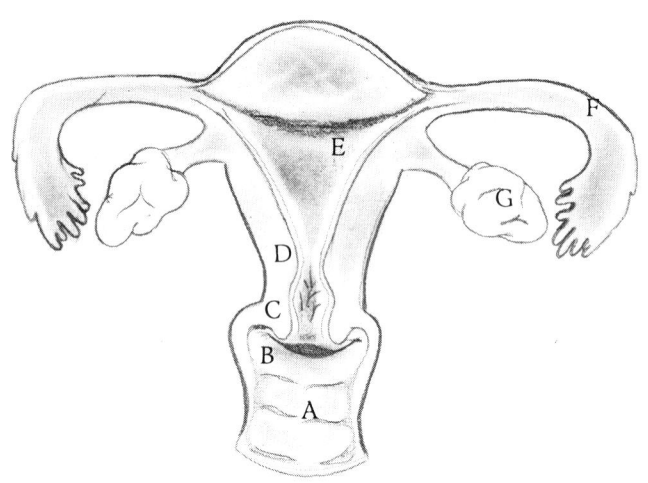

Figure 1.
The internal femal reproductive organs.
A-vagina B-external os C-cervical canal
D-internal os E-uterus F-Fallopian tube G-ovary

cells of the endometrium mixed with blood. It generally lasts 3-5 days and involves 30-80 milliliters (1-3 ounces) of this bloody discharge. The blood flows from the uterus through the cervical canal, into the vagina and out of the body.

According to Talmudic law, a woman is not considered a *niddah* unless the bleeding originates from the uterine lining and then flows out of the uterus.[22] A significant discussion exists among the commentators regarding the anatomy of the reproductive tract. Beside the historical interest, the discussion as it relates to the anatomical landmarks that define a state of *niddah* is very significant.

The Mishnah states that the blood must flow from the "inner compartment" into the "outer compartment" but need not flow out of the body to create a state of *niddah*.[23] The simple understanding of Maimonides' (1135-1204) commentary is that the blood must flow just past the external os of the cervix.[24] This understanding is adopted by Rabbi Moses Sofer (1762-1839) and is accepted as conclusive by several other authorities.[25]

Based on this approach, one may conclude that the point of demarcation is the external os and any source of bleeding internal to that point is considered "inside" according to the Talmud. Bleeding from the cervical canal could therefore also create a state of *niddah*. (Blood from the cervix outside the external os would be of no significance.) However, no explicit reference to cervical blood is made by Rabbi Sofer. Rabbi Abraham Blumenkrantz states that cervical bleeding does create a status of *niddah*.[26] However, he records no specific source for this. Rabbi Shimon Eider refers only to uterine bleeding.[27] Rabbi Aharon Pfoifer concludes unequivocally that cervical bleeding due to any cause does not create a state of *niddah*, and that only uterine bleeding is significant. As he points out, this is because cyclic shedding and bleeding occur only from the uterus, not the cervix.[28]

A second understanding of the anatomical boundaries is based on Rashi, Rabbi Shlomo Yitzhaki (1040-1105).[29] This is quoted by Rabbi Abraham Karelitz (1878-1953),[30] and places the point of demarcation somewhere in the vagina itself (before the cervix). Rabbi Shlomo Zalman Auerbach also adopts this view and even interprets Maimonides' commentary in this way, dissenting with Rabbi Sofer's interpretation.[31] Clearly, vaginal bleeding from inside this point would be of no significance, as the uterus is the only source of bleeding with halakhic import. The only question is whether cervical bleeding is of importance, as it can be viewed as part of the uterus and in the "inside compartment" according to these two approaches.

A third approach places the point of demarcation at the internal os. According to this view the woman is a *niddah* as soon as blood enters the cervical canal from the uterus and, obviously, any bleeding from the cervix would be of no significance. This opinion is quoted by Rabbi Auerbach, who rejects it.[32] As a practical matter, regardless of which opinion is adopted, cervical bleeding due to any cause does not create a state of *niddah*.[33] It is only uterine bleeding that is of halakhic significance, as the cyclic shedding and bleeding occur only from the uterus — not from the cervix.[34] Also, blood found anywhere in the vagina during an internal examination imposes a state of *niddah* unless the source of blood is known to be outside the uterus. The same applies to the spotting of undergarments.

B. Physiologic and Normal Flow

The Talmud discusses a "tube" as an exception to the principle that uterine bleeding creates a state of *niddah*. The Talmud deduces that, in order to impose a state of *niddah*, the blood must flow directly through the reproductive tract and not through some other medium or tube.[35] Thus, if a tube was inserted into the uterus and blood was withdrawn without leaking, the woman would not be a *niddah*.[36] The reason for this exemption, according to some authorities, is that *niddah* blood must be in physical contact with the reproductive tract. The tube functions as an interruption, or partition, between the flow of the blood and the tract.[37] Accordingly, even if the tube were not inserted completely into the uterine cavity but just beyond the point of demarcation (at the external os) so that the flow of blood never made contact with the "outer compartment," the woman would not be a *niddah*.[38] (If the blood is on the external surface of the tube, the woman would be a *niddah*, as there is no physical interruption between the blood and the tract.[39]) Another rationale for the exception of the tube is that the blood must flow naturally and in a normal fashion in order to create a state of *niddah*.[40] From Rabbi Auerbach's writings, it appears that this means the bleeding must be a result of natural causes and not initiated by other factors. Secondly, the actual flow must also be normal and not, for example, assisted by some other means (such as a tube). Even a naturally induced flow which is in any way abnormal is incorporated into this exemption. Therefore, a natural flow from the uterus that travels in a tube inserted just past the external os would not create a state of *niddah*. (It is not normal for the blood to flow in a tube, regardless of whether or not its egress from the uterus is part of a natural and spontaneous process.[41]) This general idea has also been developed independently by Rabbi Eliezer Waldenberg, who discusses bleeding due to fibroids in the uterus and maintains that a woman becomes a *niddah* only if the flow of blood is part of a natural and normal physiologic process that occurs spontaneously.[42]

Thus, two criteria seem to be required for bleeding to create a state of *niddah*. The bleeding must occur in the normal fashion through the reproductive tract and not, for example, through a tube. Secondly, it must be physiologic and spontaneous, that is, not caused by other factors. As will be discussed, menstruation is not the only normal process of bleeding; there can exist other factors that promote the natural physiologic response of uterine bleeding. This first understanding of the exception of the tube is the one adopted in Shulhan Arukh, the definitive Code of Jewish Law.[43]

It is significant to note that the argument could be made that the nature of the cause of bleeding is irrelevant. As long as the anatomical soure is the endometrium, or uterine lining, it is considered *niddah* bleeding by definition. It would still remain correct to require that the actual flow occur normally and unassisted — not through a tube, for example. This second requirement is the only one fairly explicitly expressed in the Talmud; the first one is not. It is this issue that is perhaps the most fundamental one for the issues discussed in this chapter. This author feels that the issue is at present inconclusive and in need of further analysis.

A third rationale which explains the exemption of the tube is that some form of sensation by the woman is required.[44] Flow in a tube occurs without the sensation of something flowing, and is therefore exempt from the Biblical laws of *niddah*, which require some kind of sensation associated with the bleeding. Still, such a woman should be a *niddah* based on rabbinic legislation. All authorities agree, however, that, with the tube scenario, the woman is not a *niddah* on either a biblical or a rabbinic level.[45] Therefore, this approach has been rejected.

C. Cervical Dilation

The Talmud discusses the case of a woman who experiences a miscarriage without any associated bleeding.[46] This phenomenon, referred to in the Talmud as a "dry birth," seems to have occurred at that time. The question is whether such an event is equated with normal delivery, which imposes ritual impurity upon the woman similar to that of *niddah*. If it is not considered a delivery, she may still be considered a *niddah* as there might have been unobserved bleeding.[47]

In the discussion regarding the latter possibility, a disagreement emerges as to whether the opening of the cervix is assumed always to be associated with bleeding.[48] Maimonides explains the authoritative view, which is that it is impossible for something to be discharged from the uterus without accompanying bleeding, though the amount of blood may be so minute so as to have gone unnoticed.[49] Other commentators explain that the mere probability that bleeding is occurring is sufficient to render the woman a definite *niddah*.[50] Alternatively, the Talmud offers an opinion that it is possible for the cervix to be opened without bleeding and, therefore, such a woman is not definitely classified as a *niddah*.[51] The Shulhan Arukh rules that the opening of the cervix is associated with bleeding. Therefore, a woman who experiences a miscarriage even within 40 days of conception (which is not considered delivery) is considered a *niddah*.[52]

Rabbi Ezekiel Landau (1713-1793) maintains that any opening of the cervix, whether internally or externally induced, qualifies as an opening.[53] This would include note only a miscarriage, but also a procedure or examination by a physician which involves the opening of the cervix. This ruling introduced for the first time the possibility of a physician inducing a state of *niddah* in the course of a medical procedure.

Rabbi Abraham Danzig (1748-1820) disagrees with Rabbi Landau.[54] However, it is not clear if he disagrees in principle or only with regard to the reality of a manual pelvic examination causing such an opening.[55] Some authorities question Rabbi Landau's view because he lacks any source.[56] The Talmudic examples all involve an obviously internal delivery or labor process. The birthing process was generally assumed to be associated with bleeding. Due to the nature of the process, the discharge of the uterine contents drags blood along. So, even if the "dry birth" was premature and not labelled technically as a delivery, it is assumed that there was bleeding. However, the simple external opening of the cervix would not normally result in bleeding.[57]

It is clear from the Talmudic and halakhic discussion that uterine bleeding does not have to occur in the context of menstruation in order to render a woman a *niddah*. Any bleeding, even if it occurs in response to some external stimulus (such as physical activity), imposes a state of *niddah*.[58] It remains questionable whether the opening of the cervix induces a state of *niddah*. While the issue remains incompletely resolved and in need of further analysis, Rabbi Landau's view is adopted in practice by many authorities, including Rabbi Feinstein.[59]

A further controversy exists over which portion of the cervix, if opened, causes a suspicion of uterine bleeding and therefore a state of *niddah*. Some hold the view that the internal os must be dilated for any concern to arise, while others maintain that dilation of even the external os causes such concern.[60] In support of the first opinion is the anatomical fact that the external os has no real connection with the uterus and, therefore, opening it cannot truly cause uterine bleeding. If the internal os remains closed, the uterus cannot be affected by the pressure of the external os being opened.[61] Rabbi Auerbach discusses this issue and concludes that the dilation need only occur at the external os to cause concern for uterine bleeding and thereby induce a state of *niddah*.[62]

Another question associated with the dilation of the cervix is the minimum diameter of the opening necessary to create a concern for bleeding. Rabbi Yosef Karo, author of the Shulhan Arukh, rules elsewhere that a narrow tube does not dilate the cervix sufficiently to stimulate bleeding.[63] Some accept this leniency with the condition that the woman perform an internal examination and that no blood is found.[64] Rabbi Feinstein accepts this view without any such condition and defines the diameter of the opening to be three quarters of an inch, or approximately 19 millimeters.[65] Others record a diameter of 13 millimeters.[66]

D. *Makkah*

The last issue we will consider is that of a *makkah* (wound). The Talmud and Shulhan Arukh rule that bleeding from a wound or lesion does not render the woman a *niddah*, even if the wound is in the uterine lining itself.[67] The exemption of *makkah* does not always require absolute knowledge that the source of bleeding is a wound. As long as the bleeding can be attributed to a wound, and it is known that the wound has the potential to leak blood, the woman is not a *niddah*.[68] However, this rule does not apply at the time that normal menstrual bleeding is expected.[69] The leniency at other times of the menstrual cycle is appropriate for women in our era as well, in spite of the fact that their periods often vary in timing.[70] Examples of wounds include fibroids, lacerations, ulcerations and inflammation.[71] The question is whether a simple abrasion or cut resulting in transient bleeding is considered a *makkah*. In this case, no physical wound existed prior to the bleeding, nor does any gross healing process ensue that might constitute a wound. Some authorities seem to consider this a *makkah*. It would appear from the halakha of hymenal bleeding discussed next that any bleeding induced by physical trauma constitutes a *makkah*.

A woman does become a *niddah* on a rabbinic level as a result of the tearing of the hymen during the first intercourse, and the normal laws of *niddah* follow.[72] On occasion, the hymen can be resistant to penetration and a surgical procedure may be required to break it. Rabbi Feinstein feels that hymenal bleeding following such a procedure does not make a woman a *niddah*. He points out that, in all cases, hymenal bleeding is really only that of *makkah*. While the rabbis nevertheless ruled that hymenal bleeding creates a state of *niddah*, they imposed this injunction only in cases of bleeding resulting from normal intercourse. In cases of instrumentation, the normal law of *makkah* takes over.[73] Even those who disagree with Rabbi Feinstein's conclusion concede that it is really a *makkah*.[74] Therefore, any instrumentation that causes bleeding falls under the category of *makkah*.[75]

Rabbi Feinstein elsewhere seems to be of the opinion that bleeding from the uterus caused by instrumentation renders the woman a *niddah*. He discusses the use of some kind of an electric instrument, perhaps a laser, in the treatment of fibroids which have enlarged because of a pregnancy. He claims that if the instrument itself causes bleeding from the uterus not at the site of the wound or lesion, the woman is a *niddah*.[76] The specific case involved the seven clean days, and therefore, they would be cancelled as a result. Although the cause was clearly traumatic, Rabbi Feinstein did not consider it a *makkah* because the bleeding was not from an actual lesion. Elsewhere, however, he implies that instrumentation by the physician *is* considered a *makkah*.[77] Doctor Abraham understands Rabbi Feinstein's view in this way as well.[78] The issue discussed there was that of cervical dilation.[1] Rabbi Feinstein was not concerned if the diameter of the opening was less than three quarters of an inch, as previously discussed. Therefore, if there is bleeding and the physician claims it is due to the instrument, Rabbi Feinstein seems to consider it wound-bleeding, or *makkah*.

It would appear that bleeding caused by *any* physical trauma should not create a state of *niddah*. As mentioned previously, both Rabbis Auerbach and Waldenberg seem to define *niddah* bleeding as being a natural and spontaneous physiologic process. Any traumatic bleeding is, by its very nature, not a naturally occurring process. For this reason, Rabbi Auerbach claims that even if the same arteries that bleed during menstruation are bleeding as a result of *makkah*, the woman is not a *niddah*.[79] In other words, wound-bleeding falls under the principle derived from the "tube." Such bleeding is not considered the normal mode of bleeding. Furthermore, Rabbi Karelitz, in a response to Dr. Taub, delineates the various categories of uterine bleeding. He states that bleeding resulting from a cut in the uterine lining is a *makkah*. His argument is that only bleeding from the uterus that is unique to the uterus creates a state of *niddah*. This includes menstruation and the birthing process. However, bleeding that results from other causes, which may similarly result in bleeding from other organs of the body — such as abrasions and lacerations — does not create a state of *niddah*.[80] A woman with this type of bleeding is considered to have a *makkah* and is therefore not to be considered a *niddah*. Elsewhere, Rabbi Karelitz also explains the exemption of *makkah* to be that such bleeding is not considered the normal mode of bleeding from the uterus. Rabbi Pfoifer quotes this latter notion from Rabbi Karelitz as he explains the exemption of *makkah*.[81] Both concepts presented here should be applicable to any traumatic bleeding.

While traumatic bleeding may not create a state of *niddah*, it is still significant for a woman beginning the sequence of seven clean days. All bleeding must cease prior to the seven days to enable the woman to realistically and accurately perform internal examinations. Even bleeding due to a *makkah* prevents a woman from discerning whether she is also still bleeding due to her regular period. This also applies to the first of the seven days (if bleeding occurs then, the seven day sequence is cancelled and an attempt to restart it is reinitiated.) Therefore, the internal examination on the first day must be accurate and discernible as well. If she experiences wound bleeding anytime after the first day, that bleeding is insignificant and is disregarded totally. Rabbi Feinstein makes note of these qualifications in regard to the general exemption of *makkah*.[83] It should be noted that if the trauma was induced by a physician during an examination or procedure, he or she may be relied upon to categorically claim that all the bleeding that was observed was traumatic in origin. Bleeding that occurs sometime after the physician has completed the procedure cannot be assumed categorically to be entirely traumatic in origin, even if the physician claims it to be. Therefore, all bleeding would have to cease prior to beginning the seven clean days, as already explained.[84]

THE GYNECOLOGICAL EXAM

We now turn to various gynecological examinations and their possible impact on a patient's *niddah* status. A preliminary word, however, is necessary on the issue of modesty.

Women who observe the laws of *niddah* generally maintain a commitment to laws of modesty that run counter to contemporary norms. Thus, for example, a male doctor should be aware that a religious woman would be very uncomfortable being left alone with a man — even her doctor — in a closed room, even before the physical examination has begun. Some patients may be intimidated to ask for a nurse to be present, thinking that the doctor might take offense. Here, the doctor should take the initiative in guaranteeing that a third person is present in the room, or that the door to an adjacent occupied room is left open.

Based on the preceding presentations, it is possible to apply the four principles developed to specific diagnostic procedures in the female patient. The diagnostic procedures used during the fertility investigation are designed to follow a logical order and are generally performed beginning with the least invasive procedure and ending with the most invasive. Each procedure is designed to examine one or more possible causes of infertility.

A. Pelvic Exam

The pelvic exam includes speculum and bimanual exams, which are aimed at assessing abnormalities of the vagina, cervix, uterus, Fallopian tubes and ovaries. Infections, tumors, lacerations and structural abnormalities can be diagnosed. The speculum exam allows for visualization of the cervix, at which time a Papanicolaou (Pap) smear is often performed (Figure 2). The Pap smear involves collecting samples of cells from the area around the external os and cervical canal and observing them under a microscope. A spatula of plastic or wood is used to abrade or scrape the external cervical surface for cells. A thin cotton swab or bristle tipped brush is often used to obtain cells from the cervical canal. Information regarding infections and tumors can be gleaned from a Pap smear. The bimanual exam involves the insertion of two of the physician's fingers into the vagina until the cervix is felt. A second hand is used

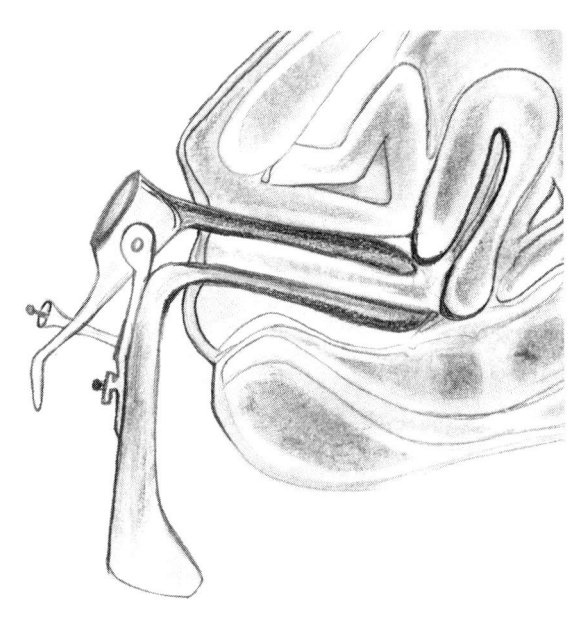

Figure 2.
The Speculum Exam

externally to feel the uterus and adjacent structures (Figure 3).[85]

The pelvic exam (including the Pap smear) poses absolutely no problem regarding the laws of *niddah*. The bimanual and speculum exams do not involve dilation of the cervix and do not, in general, cause any bleeding. If perchance they do, the bleeding does not anatomically involve the uterine lining in any way. If the physician makes contact with the cervix manually or with the speculum, no penetration of the cervical canal occurs. Bleeding from the cervix outside the external os is certainly not of significance. This basic view is the conclusion of many authorities.[86]

A Pap smear that involves inserting a cotton swab or brush into the cervical canal is also of no

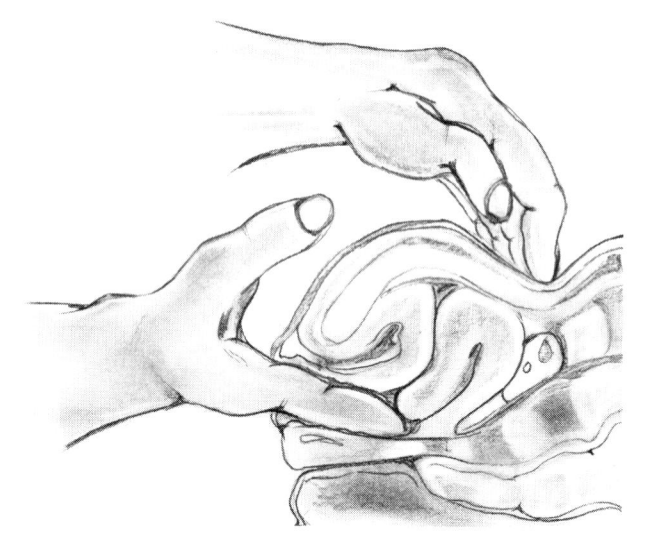

Figure 3.
The Bimanual Exam

concern. The cervix is not dilated to any significant extent if at all. Rabbi Feinstein's minimum measure of dilation is approximately 19 millimeters. The external os is normally open approximately three millimeters in diameter.[87] Therefore, the concern of somehow stimulating bleeding from the uterus by dilating the external os is not a realistic one. Also, according to many authorities, it is the dilation of the internal os that is of significance. If the scraping of cells from the cervical canal produces bleeding, it is not bleeding that creates a state of *niddah* because, as already discussed, only bleeding from the uterine lining constitutes bleeding of a *niddah*. Although Rabbi Blumenkrantz seems to be concerned about cervical bleeding, this does not seem to represent the predominant view.[88] Dr. Abraham also dismisses the Pap smear as a reason for concern, based purely on anatomy.[89] Furthermore, cervical bleeding caused by a Pap smear might be equivalent to a *makkah*, or wound. As was already discussed, bleeding from a *makkah* does not render a woman a *niddah*.[90]

The Pap smear is usually not performed during menstruation. If it is performed during the last six of the seven clean days, there is no need for concern and the days are unaffected. However, if performed prior to the onset of the seven clean days, when all bleeding must have ceased, a woman cannot begin this sequence if any bleeding due to any cause is occurring internally through the vagina. This is because, as explained earlier, the internal examination cannot be accurate in determining that no further uterine bleeding is occurring. If all the bleeding that occurs, however, is observed by a physician to be entirely from outside the uterus, then the seven clean days may commence normally. Bleeding that occurs sometime after the physician has completed the procedure or examination cannot be assumed to be coming from outside the uterus, even if this is the physician's claim. These qualifications apply to the first of the seven days as well. Bleeding from a *makkah* during the remaining six days is of no import. Rabbi Feinstein makes this point clear, based on other authorities.[91]

B. Post-Coital Testing (PCT)

This test involves the collection of a mucus specimen from the cervical canal. The mucus is examined for infection as well as for quality and quantity. Cervical mucus is important for sperm motility and penetration. The test is an indication of the function of the ovaries, as hormones produced by the ovaries affect the nature of the mucus. The examination is performed at the time of ovulation, which is approximately two weeks after menstruation. The patient should have had intercourse within 12 to 24 hours before, hence the name 'post-coital.' A syringe attached to a soft catheter is used to aspirate mucus from the canal. The exam can be performed in conjunction with the pelvic exam and Pap smear.[92] No dilation of the external os occurs to any significant degree. No bleeding should occur and any that does is not uterine. Due to the required timing of the test, the PCT normally does not occur immediately before or during the seven day period. If it does, the same qualifications metioned in section A apply.

C. Cervical Dilation and Endometrial Biopsy

The dilation of the cervical canal at both the external os and internal os is performed to gain access to the uterine cavity. This allows an endometrial biopsy to be performed. The biopsy is aimed at obtaining tissue, or cells, from the uterine lining. This provides information about both ovarian function and uterine capacity for implantation. It can, for example, diagnose endometritis, or inflammation of the uterine lining. It is best performed one or two days before the onset of menstruation.[93]

The biopsy is performed by visualizing the cervix through a speculum, then grasping its anterior (upper) lip (around the external os) with a wire hook, or tenaculum, in such a way as to avoid the blood supply to the cervix. (However, superficial bleeding from the cervix can occur.) On occasion, the cervix must first be dilated with a thin probe, or dilator, which can measure 7-11 mm in diameter. A curette, or scraping device is then inserted into the uterus to scrape off cells from the lining (Figure 4). The dilators and curettes can be hollow, thus allowing for blood to egress. Bleeding is a normal occurrence after any type of endometrial biopsy and can last from a couple of hours to one or two days.[94] Newer instruments have recently been developed which allow a biopsy to be taken without grasping the cervix and without forcefully dilating the cervical canal.

Cervical dilation does not create a state of *niddah*. Any bleeding from the cervix at the area of the external os or the cervical canal is anatomically not *niddah* bleeding. The dilation of the internal os is insufficient to render the woman a *niddah*. While all authorities agree that the opening of the internal os, even in the absence of bleeding, causes a woman to become a *niddah*, Rabbi Feinstein has established the minimum diameter for such dilation as 19 mm. Clearly, the dilation performed during biopsy is comfortably less than this minimum diameter. It is also less than Rabbi Blumenkrantz's 12.7 mm cutoff. The bleeding that results from the actual biopsy may be problematic. The blood that flows from the uterus through a hollow curette out of the cervical canal does not, according to most opinions, impose a state of *niddah*, as we have seen with the principle of the tube. The blood that exits around the curette as well as bleeding that ensues sometime after the procedure is completed may or may not create a state of *niddah*. This depends on the discussion earlier regarding the possible requirement of a natural and spontaneous

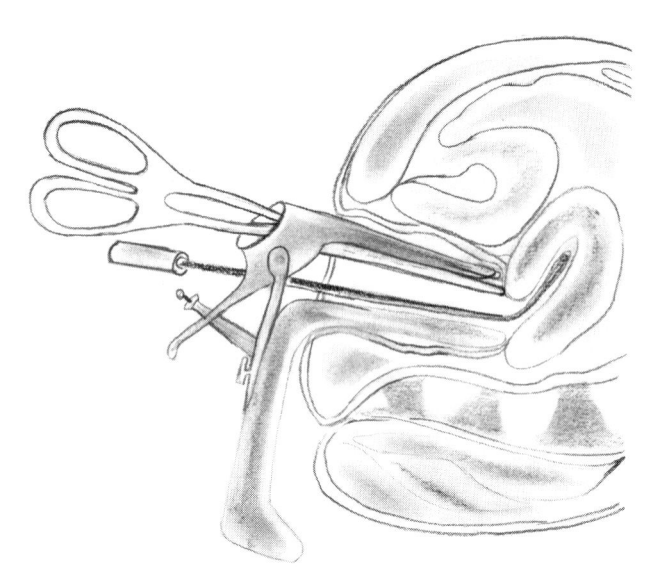

Figure 4.
Endometrial Biopsy

flow and whether instrumentation-induced bleeding is exempted based on the principle of *makkah*. This author feels that the issue remains inconclusive.[95]

Since the biopsy is performed very near to the expected date of menstruation, the practicality of intimate relations with one's spouse may not exist. The laws of *niddah* proscribe intercourse for a period of time immediately prior to the anticipated onset of bleeding as a safeguard against having relations once the period has begun.[96] Depending on the woman's natural cycle, there may still exist one or two nights during which intercourse would be permissible. Also, once menstruation begins, the five initial days before the seven clean days begin. They do not begin with the uterine bleeding from the biopsy. Since biopsies are sometimes performed just at the onset of menstruation, attention should be directed at discerning when the menstrual bleeding begins. Again, the qualifications of beginning the seven clean days apply here as already detailed in section A.

It should be noted that some authorities, including Rabbi Auerbach as quoted by Dr. Abraham, express concern regarding bleeding that occurs during or following any procedure performed around the expected time of menstruation. Their concern is that the bleeding resulting from such a procedure may actually represent menstrual bleeding if penetration of the uterine cavity with an instrument occurred. Therefore, a state of *niddah* may have been induced by the procedure. Again, this would only be of concern if the procedure were performed at the time of the expected menstrual flow, and only if bleeding were noticed by either the physician or the patient.[97] As always, a competent rabbinic authority must be consulted for practical halakhic decisions.

D. Hysterosalpingogram (HSG)

In order to visualize the uterus and Fallopian tubes by x-ray, a dye must first be injected into the uterine cavity and Fallopian tubes. This procedure gives the doctor information about tubal architecture and function. If the dye is seen to spill out of the tubes and into the pelvis, this verifies that the tubes are patent, or open. If an obstruction exists, it can be found. On occasion, the HSG can be therapeutic as well as diagnostic, by overcoming an obstruction that existed.[98]

The HSG is performed after menstrual bleeding has ceased, but before ovulation has occurred (so as not to inadvertently interrupt a pregnancy). A speculum is inserted in order to expose the cervix. Depending on the type of instillation system used, a tenaculum may be used to grasp the cervix. Dye is instilled into the uterine cavity by passing a catheter or cannula past the internal os. The catheters are very thin — on the order of 3 mm, or equal to the diameter of the cervical canal's natural opening (Figure 5).[99]

After an HSG, bleeding generally occurs. Usually, it represents leakage of the radiographic dye from the uterus and vagina. This fluid is blood-tinged, either from contact with the endometrium or from mixing with blood that oozes from the cervix after the tenaculum is withdrawn.[100] The bleeding that occurs from the cervix does not create a state of *niddah* based on anatomical considerations. The bleeding that is uterine in origin may create a state of *niddah*. While it should be considered traumatic in nature, we have already detailed that this may not necessarily mitigate a state of *niddah*. This issue, again, remains inconclusive. If any dilation of the cervix occurs, it is always well below the 19 mm defined by Rabbi Feinstein.[101]

To begin the seven clean days, the same qualifications mentioned in section A are operative here as well.

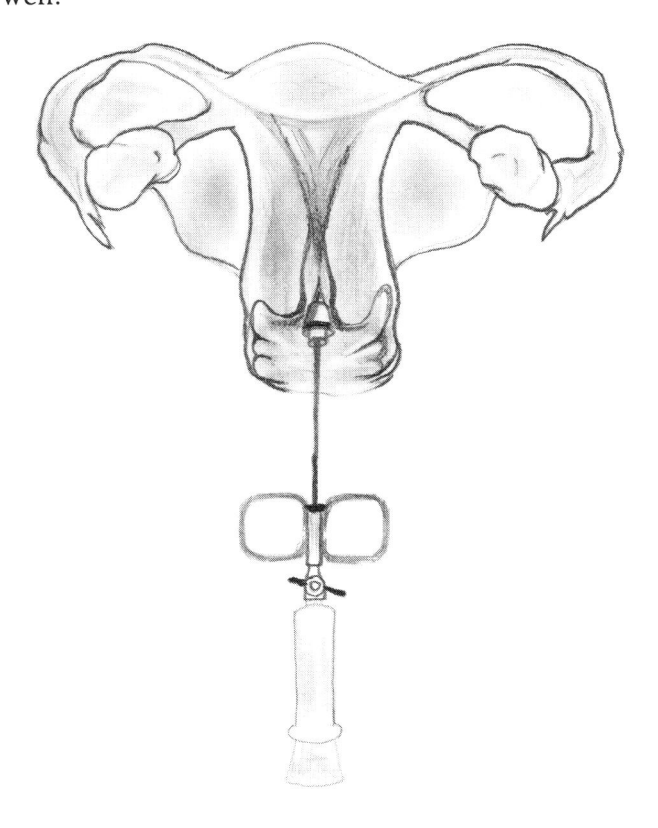

Figure 5.
Hysterosalpingogram

E. Laparoscopy and Hysteroscopy

Laparoscopy is a surgical procedure which involves making a small incision in or just below the navel. A thin telescope is inserted through this incision into the abdominal cavity. This allows the surgeon to visualize directly the ovaries, Fallopian tubes and uterus for abnormalities. It detects physical or mechanical obstructions around the tubes such as adhesions and endometriosis (sites of uterine tissue growth outside the uterus). During laparoscopy, dye may be instilled into the uterus and through the tubes as in an HSG. Using special instruments such as a laser, many pelvic reconstructive procedures, including the removal of endometriosis or repair of the Fallopian tubes, can now be performed during laparoscopy.[102]

Laparoscopy is almost always performed under general anesthesia. First, a pelvic exam is performed. A tenaculum is then used to grasp the cervix and a cannula is inserted into the uterus. This enhances positioning of the uterus for proper visualization through the laparoscope. It also allows dye to be injected through the Fallopian tubes during the procedure. Often, hysteroscopy is performed in conjunction with laparoscopy. It involves the insertion of a thin telescope (hysteroscope) of 6-10 mm in diameter past the internal cervical os. The uterus is distended with liquid or carbon dioxide gas and its internal surfaces are visualized directly. Occasionally, biopsy or other operative procedures are performed through the hysteroscope.[103]

Bleeding from the cervix caused by the tenaculum is anatomically not *niddah* bleeding. The dilation of the cervix that occurs with the cannula is well under the limits established. The only concern would be regarding uterine bleeding caused by its insertion. The issue, again, is whether such bleeding would be considered that of a *makkah*. This point remains, once again, in need of further analysis. Likewise, in hysteroscopy, the telescope is a relatively small diameter. Of course, after the procedure, the seven clean days can begin only under the qualifications described in section A.

F. Ultrasound

A vaginal ultrasound is helpful in visualizing the uterus and ovaries. A probe is inserted into the vagina up to the cervix, but not beyond (Figure 6). It

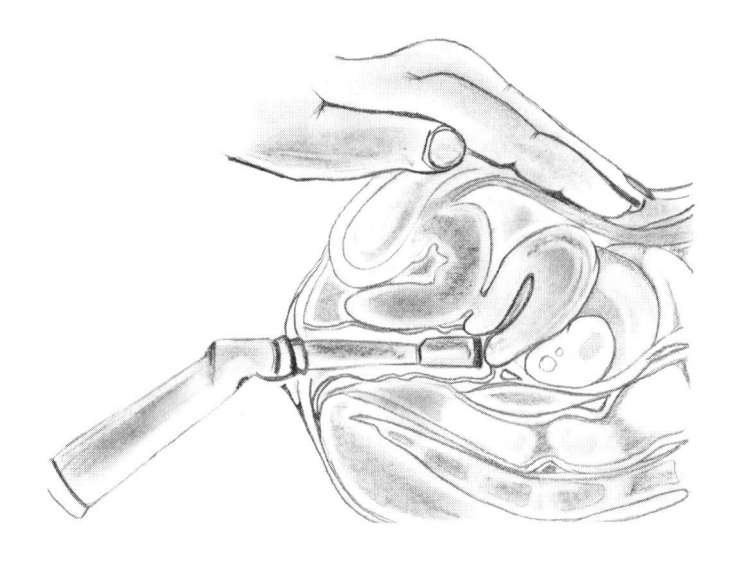

Figure 6.
Vaginal ultrasound

does not create a state of *niddah*, as anatomically it does not enter the uterus or even the cervical canal. Bleeding generally does not occur. If it does, the same qualifications regarding the initiation of the seven clean days already established in section A apply here, as well.

It should be noted that if, during any of these procedures, the physician notices blood unrelated to the procedures, the woman is assumed to be a *niddah*.[104] It is no different than if she had examined herself and found blood on a cloth. This is true regardless of the timing within the cycle.

SABBATH CONSIDERATIONS

Lastly, we turn to the issue of performing certain tests or procedures on the Sabbath. The ideas developed here apply equally to the Jewish holidays, such as Passover. The Jewish Sabbath — beginning at sunset Friday evening and ending close to one hour after sunset Saturday evening — is one of the fundamental pillars of halakhic Judaism. Various Biblical and rabbinic restrictions apply during the Sabbath. Therefore, both the physician and patient should be aware of how certain diagnostic procedures might be affected by the Sabbath.

It is more than likely that almost all the procedures previously described will not be scheduled for Saturdays. Also, the patient can easily schedule the procedures during non-holiday times, as these are not emergency procedures and their performance would invariably pose halakhic problems.

The diagnostic procedures that are bound by tight scheduling are the post-coital test (PCT) and endometrial biopsy. During certain types of therapy, the performance of diagnostic ultrasound and blood testing may also require scheduling on the Sabbath. However, scheduling even these procedures for a Saturday or holiday is halakhically unacceptable. The Sabbath cannot be suspended for non-life-threatening conditions. This is certainly true regarding Biblical prohibitions. Non-life-threatening conditions can mitigate the observance of rabbinic ordinances, but this is not absolute. The nature of the ordinance and the exact nature of the condition are the two factors that need to be considered. Although infertility is a serious condition, related diagnostic and therapeutic procedures do not automatically justify overriding rabbinic restrictions.[105]

In any case, the procedures in question may very likely require Biblical violations, such as the driving of a car. The use of electrical equipment may be another problem. Performing the actual PCT on the Sabbath is probably a rabbinic violation, while the biopsy may be a Biblical one. These procedures can usually be rescheduled for a month when no conflict will exist with the Sabbath. The Sabbath is generally suspended only when no alternatives to its violation exist.

Two diagnostic procedures not previously mentioned might also have to be done on Saturdays and holidays: BBT (basal body temperature) and LH (luteinizing hormone) testing. BBT is a person's temperature while at rest. Due to the hormonal effects of ovulation, a woman's BBT rises approximately 1° F at midcycle and remains elevated during the luteal, or second half of the cycle (though not all women are equally sensitive to this effect). The infertile woman who uses this technique to detect ovulation generally measures her temperature orally every morning before engaging in any activity, and then records it on a chart for the duration of one complete cycle. Besides yielding some information regarding the occurence of ovulation, it is occasionally used for purposes of scheduling a PCT and/or endometrial biopsy.[106]

The problem with BBT testing is one of measuring, for taking measurements and weights on the Sabbath is a rabbinic prohibition. (One reason given relates to the close association between commerce and measurements and the fact that commerce is prohibited on the Sabbath and holidays.) Rabbi Waldenberg, however, categorically permits an infertility patient to measure her temperature on the Sabbath with a standard mercury thermometer. His rationale is that measuring one's temperature has absolutely no association with commerce and is therefore not equivalent to the measuring restricted by the rabbis.[107] Rabbi Feinstein and Rabbi Auerbach make this point as well.[108] Another line of reasoning, presented by Rabbi Waldenberg, is that measuring is only prohibited if it involves a physical structure of some kind such as a table, and this is not the case with one's temperature. Although BBT measurements are permitted on the Sabbath, one must be careful not to perform associated tasks — such as smearing, squeezing or writing — which involve their own Biblical prohibitions. If the temperature is measured rectally, one must avoid applying vaseline to the thermometer. If necessary, the thermometer may be dipped into vaseline, but it should not be spread or smeared across the thermometer. It is permissible to immerse the thermometer into alcohol only if it is to be used subsequently on that Sabbath. One can wipe off the alcohol with a cotton ball but should not soak or moisten a cotton ball with alcohol to clean the thermomoeter. It is permissible to shake down the mercury column for use on the Sabbath.[109] Finally, recording the temperature in writing is absolutely prohibited, even with a pencil. One must wait until after the Sabbath, or use prepared number pieces.

In recent years, BBT charting has largely been replace by a more precise procedure, which involves the measurement of LH levels in the urine. (LH is the hormone that triggers ovulation. If it is absent or low, ovulation is not occurring.) In a normal cycling woman, the development of a ripe egg within the ovary signals the pituitary gland to secrete large amounts of LH. This hormonal "surge" precedes ovulation by 12-36 hours and occurs around midcycle, or fourteen days before the onset of menstruation. The urinary LH kit allows a woman to anticipate her ovulation by indicating when the LH surge is occurring, since LH in the blood circulation is rapidly excreted in the urine. The test involves dipping a small, color-coded stick in a sample of urine. The color changes that result correspond to different levels of LH in the urine. Knowing when ovulation is occuring is useful in order to time intercourse accurately. It is also useful to time such procedures as post-coital testing, endometrial biopsy and artificial insemination.

The problem regarding LH testing is one of dying or coloring. (The process of dying leather, for example, constitutes a Biblical violation of the Sabbath. Some forms of dying and coloring are rabbinic in nature, and still others are permissible.) Rabbi Neuwirth quotes opinions who allow the use of dipsticks on the Sabbath. One mitigating factor is that the color changes are transient in that they are only really noticeable for a brief period of time, after which they fade.[110] Another reason for leniency is that, unlike the dying of leather and other materials, the patient isn't really interested in the colored paper per se, but only in the information it provides.[111] Furthermore, the method used is somewhat indirect, in that the patient isn't applying a dye or color but only immersing the stick in the urine, which then brings about color changes.[112]

However, Rabbi Neuwirth also quotes Rabbi Auerbach's view, which is somewhat skeptical about the leniency regarding dipsticks. Rabbi Auerbach recognizes that the patient is really interested only in the information obtained from the dipstick and not in having some colored material. He argues, however, that since the color changes in the stick are of interest, for whatever reason, this might be sufficient to constitute a Sabbath violation of dying and coloring. Rabbi Auerbach concludes, therefore, that it is preferable to effect a color change somewhat indirectly by having the urine spread through the stick on its own without being dipped in.[113] One can do this by dipping the edge of the stick in the urine sample, and allowing the urine to then naturally diffuse through the stick. It should be noted that the cup of urine itself is considered *muktzeh*, or sequestered on the Sabbath from being handled and moved, once it has been used for testing.[114] Therefore, once the container has been put down, it should not be manipulated further unless its location is such that people would be annoyed by its presence and odor.[115] The insertion of the dipstick does not pose a *muktzeh* problem.

CONCLUSION

We return to our opening comment concerning the relevance of these religious laws to the overall fertility therapy. Health professionals who are not personally familiar with (let alone committed to) halakhic observance can find it incredible that such religious restrictions could be allowed to frustrate the therapy if the couple had a real desire to conceive. Such value judgments have no place in the patient-doctor relationship.

Therapy must address the patient as a whole, and the religious commitments of a patient may be at the core of his or her personal identity. Understanding the restrictions imposed by these commitments can help the physician construct a therapy protocol best suited for the patient at hand.

Acknowledgments

The author would like to express his appreciation to Rabbi Hershel Schachter, Rosh Yeshiva and Nathan and Vivian Fink Distinguished Professor of Talmud at Yeshiva University's Rabbi Isaac Elchanan Theological Seminary. Rabbi Schachter reviewed the halakhic material of the text, though not all the opinions expressed within are necessarily consistent with his.

The author would also like to express his appreciation to Rabbi Tzvi Harari, a fellow of Yeshiva University's Joseph and Caroline Gruss Kollel Elyon (post-graduate program), for his research assistance.

114 BE FRUITFUL AND MULTIPLY

NOTES

1. Leviticus 15:19, 25.
2. Mishneh Torah (Code of Maimonides), Hilkhot Issurei Bi'ah 6:2.
3. Niddah 68a. Cf. Mishneh Torah, Hilkhot Issurei Bi'ah, 6:20.
4. Leviticus 15:28; Shulhan Arukh, Yoreh De'ah 196:1. Cf. Mishneh Torah, Hilkhot Issurei Bi'ah 6:7,8,11. The examination is referred to as the Hefsek Taharah, or conclusion or interruption in (a state of) purity.
5. Mishneh Torah, Hilkhot Issurei Bi'ah, 7:13.
6. Ibid., 4:12. Cf. Leviticus 18:19.
7. Ibid., 7:13.
8. Niddah 57b. Cf. Resp. Tzofnat Pane'ah, no. 7.
9. Pithei Teshuvah on Shulhan Arukh, Yoreh De'ah 183:1 subscript 1, Cf. Rabbi Aharon Pfoifer, Kitzur Shulhan Arukh, Hikhot Niddah, chapter 5 and Rabbi Feivel Cohen, Badei Hashulhan 183:1, subscript 5.
  The second type of sensation mentioned is one that women at present are not sensitive to or aware of and, therefore, it is not an accurate way of determining whether a Biblical or rabbinic state of *niddah* has been created. Also, others suggest that the second type of sensation is one of pain or discomfort associated with the bleeding. Cf. Darkei Teshuvah on Shulhan Arukh, Yoreh De'ah 183:1 subscripts 5,6.
10. Cf. Talmud, Niddah 66a, and Mishneh Torah Hilkhot Issurei Bi'ah, 11:4.
11. Ibid.
12. Ibid. This period is referred to as the *shiva nekkiyim*, or the seven "clean" days.
13. Mishneh Torah Hilkhot Issurei Bi'ah 6:11,13 and 7:13. Cf. Shulhan Arukh, Yoreh De'ah, 197:1,3,4.

Diagnostic Evaluations 115

14. Shulhan Arukh, Yoreh De'ah 140:1.
15. Ibid. 196:10.
16. Rama, Gloss on Shulhan Arukh, Yoreh De'ah, 196:11.
17. Ibid.
18. Niddah 33a,b.
19. Rama, Yoreh De'ah 196:11.
20. Shulhan Arukh, Yoreh De'ah 196:4,5,6.
21. Cf. F.G. Cunningham, P.C. MacDonald and N.F. Gant, *Williams Obstetrics*, 18th edition (1989), pp. 871-887 and *Current Obstetrics and Gynecologic Diagnosis and Treatment*, e. M.L. Pernoll, 7th edition (1991), p. 42.
22. Niddah 17b; and Shulhan Arukh, Yoreh De'ah 183:1.
23. Niddah 40a.
24. Mishneh Torah, Hilkhot Issurei Bi'ah 5:2-5.
25. Resp. Hatam Sofer, Yoreh De'ah, no. 167; Kitzur Shulhan Arukh, Hilkhot Niddah, chapter 1, section 1, pp 83-84, and Rabbi Shmuel Wosner, Shiurei Sheivet HaLevi, Hilkhot Niddah 183:2.
26. Rabbi Avraham Blumenkrantz, Gefen Poriah (1984), 1:14, p. 9 and endnote 48, p. 190.
27. Hilkhot Niddah, pp. 4-5.
28. Kitzur Shulhan Arukh Hilkhot Niddah, chapter 1, section 1, pp. 83-84. Cf. *Current Obstetrics and Gynecologic Diagnosis and Treatment*, ed. M.L. Pernoll, 7th edition (1991), p. 42. Maimonides seems to define the organ of bleeding as the one in which fetal development occurs. This implies that only the uterus itself — not the cervix — would be of halakhic significance. Cf. Mishneh Torah, Hilkhot Issurei Bi'ah 5:3; Tosafot, Niddah 17b, s.v. vedam ha'aliyah, and Beit Yosef on Tur Shulhan Arukh, Yoreh De'ah 183.
29. Rashi, Niddah, 41b.
30. Sefer Hazon Ish, Yoreh De'ah 92:27,28.
31. *Noam*, vol. 7, pp. 162-165. Cf. vol. 8, p. 275.

32. Ibid. pp. 167-172. Cf. Sidrei Taharah on Shulhan Arukh, Yoreh De'ah 194:26 who makes reference to such an opinion and disproves it convincingly.
33. Kitzur Shulhan Arukh, Hilkhot Niddah, section 1:1.
34. Ibid. chapter 4, section 5. and Cf. footnote 7 and section 1.
35. Niddah 21b, 57b.
36. Ibid. 21b.
37. Rashi, Niddah 21b. Cf. *Noam*, vol. 7, pp. 138-145 for a discussion by Rabbi Auerbach.
38. *Noam*, vol. 7, pp. 143-144.
39. Ibid. p. 144.
40. Rabbenu Asher's commentary to Niddah, chapter 3, section 2. Cf. *Noam*, vol. 7, pp. 146-154.
41. *Noam*, vol. 7, pp. 145-146.
42. Resp. Tzitz Eleizer, XVII, 37. Cf. index to no. 37. This view is further reinforced by Rabbi Yaakov Ettlinger (1798-1871) in Sefer Arukh L'Ner, Niddah 21b. He also seems to require that the entire flow occur in a normal fashion and not just initiated by a natural cause. He argues that the lack of contact between the blood and reproductive tract is not normal.
43. Shulhan Arukh, Yoreh De'ah 188:3.
44. Hidushei Haran, Niddah 57b.
45. Sidrei Taharah on Shulhan Arukh, Yoreh De'ah 190:1, and *Noam*, vol. 7, pp. 142-143.
46. Niddah 21a,b.
47. Rashi, Niddah 21b.
48. Niddah 21a,b.
49. Rambam's Peirush HaMishnayot (Maimonides' commentary on the Mishnah), Niddah, chapter 3, 21a. An alternative understanding is that the amount of blood may be microscopic and, therefore, not visible. However, Rabbi Hershel Schachter mentioned to this au-

thor that this is unlikely since any item which is microscopic is generally considered indignificant in terms of halakha. Cf. Iggrot Moshe, Yoreh De'ah 2:146.
50. Sefer Hazon Ish, Yoreh De'ah 215, Niddah 17b. Cf. Hidushei HaRitvah, Niddah 18b, 21a.
51. Hidushei HaRashba, Niddah 21a. Cf. Hidushei HaMeiri, Niddah 21a.
52. Shulhan Arukh, Yoreh De'ah 188:3 and 194:2.
53. Resp. Nodah Bi'Yehudah, vol. 2, Yoreh De'ah, no. 120.
54. Binat Adam, section 23.
55. Resp. Avnei Nezer, Yoreh De'ah 224. Cf. Resp. Iggrot Moshe, Yoreh De'ah, 1:83; Rabbi Feinstein also maintains that Rabbi Danzig does not argue with Rabbi Landau's principle.
56. Sefer Hazon Ish, Yoreh De'ah, section 83.
57. Maimonides' explanation cited before (note 49) also emphaized that the discharge of the contents of the uterus is always associated with bleeding. Similarly, Rashi seems to imply that only the opening of the cervix during the birth process involves bleeding. Cf. Rashi on Niddah
58. Shulhan Arukh, Yoreh De'ah 183:1 and Taz's commentary, subscript 1.
59. Resp. Iggrot Moshe, Yoreh De'ah 1:83. Cf. 1:89 and Arukh HaShulhan, Yoreh De'ah,188:51. A disagreement exists as to whether Rabbi Yosef Karo (1488-1575), author of the Shulhan Arukh, held the view of Rabbi Landau. He seems to accept it for he questions the exemption of the previously discussed tube because of the fear that the opening of the cervix by the tube will result in bleeding — albeit it is an external process of opening.
See Beit Yosef on Tur, Yoreh De'ah 188. The sugges-

tion has been made that the withdrawal of an instrument inserted into the uterus is equivalent to something being discharged from the uterus. See Resp. Beit Yitzhak, Yoreh De'ah, 2:14. However, this is still not the equivalent of a specific process that involves bleeding — namely, labor and delivery in some form. Based on this presentation, the dilation or opening of the cervix by a physician constituting a valid cause of woman becoming a *niddah* is dependent on a major disagreement amongst the authorities.
60. Shi'urei Sheivet HaLevi, Hilkhot Niddah 188:3 subscript 4; Resp. Beit Yitzhak, Yoreh De'ah 2:14.
61. Kitzur Shulhan Arukh, Hilkhot Nidah, chapter 1, section 3, pp. 85-86. Rabbi Pfoifer points out that Rabbi Feinstein also seems to accept this view. He feels, however, that in practice, one should be stringent since it is a valid dispute.
62. *Noam*, vol. 7, pp. 168-174.
63. Beit Yosef to Tur, Shulhan Arukh, Yoreh De'ah 188. Cf. Hidushei HaMeiri, Niddah 21a.
64. Resp. Avnei Nezer, Yoreh De'ah, 224.
65. Resp. Iggrot Moshe, Orah Haim, 3:100. Cf. Nishmat Avraham, Yoreh De'ah 194:4, and footnote 55.
Rabbi Feinstein's reason for leniency in terms of the diameter is partly based on the fact that Rabbi Landau's principle is a disputed one. In addition, the basic premise of bleeding being associated with any kind of opening of the cervix as presented in the Talmud is a debate among authorities. Cf. Iggrot Moshe, Yoreh De'ah, vol.1, no.89.
66. Gefen Poriah, chapter I, endnote 68, p. 194. Rabbi Blumenkrantz quotes Rabbi Feinstein's measurement as one half of an inch, which is 13 mm, approximately. This author has not found this measurement in Rabbi

Feinstein's responsa. Cf. Kitzur Shulhan Arukh Hilkhot Niddah, chapter 1, section 3, pp. 87-88 where Rabbi Pfoifer concludes that the leniency of these measurements is only appropriate vis-à-vis the dilation of the external os and not the internal os. Since the basic notion of dilation of the external causing bleeding is a questionable one, one can be lenient. Any dilation of the internal os, however, raises concern about bleeding from the uterus, since some opinions maintain that the minimum diameter is very small (the diameter of a match).

Cf. Shi'urei Sheivet HaLevi, Hilkhot Niddah 188:3 subscript 4 and 188:6 subscript 5. According to Rabbi Feinstein himself, however, it is the dilation of the internal os that stimulates bleeding. Thus, it would seem that one need not be concerned, even with regard to the dilation of the internal os if it was less than 19mm and no bleeding was noticed by the physician or patient.

67. Niddah 16a.; Shulhan Arukh, Yoreh De'ah 187:5 and Shakh's commentary there, subscript 17. Cf. Pithei Teshuvah there, subscript 22.
68. Rama, Yoreh De'ah, 187:5. Cf. Shulhan Arukh, Yoreh De'ah 196:10.
69. Ibid. in Rama and Shakh's commentary to Rama, subscript 26.
70. Badei HaShulhan 187:8.
71. Cf. Rabbi Avraham Blumenkrantz, Gefen Poriah (1984), 1:14, p. 9 and Rabbi Shimon Eider, Hilkhot Niddah, p. 5.
72. Niddah 64b,65b; Shulhan Arukh, Yoreh De'ah 193:1.
73. Resp. Iggrot Moshe, Yoreh De'ah 1:87.
74. Cf. Nishmat Avraham, Yoreh De'ah 193:2.
75. In some cases, the tearing of the hymen results in a

laceration that requires healing, so that a *makkah* was created that remains after the initial trauma. Therefore, a superficial laceration may not be exempt. Cf. Cunningham, MacDonald and Grant, *Williams Obstetrics*, p. 874.

The fact that this type of wound is transient is not a reason to mitigate its status as a *makkah*, though this has been suggested as the explanation as to why hymenal bleeding is exempt. Cf. Sidrei Taharah on Shulhan Arukh, Yoreh De'ah, 193:1.

76. Resp. Iggrot Moshe, Yoreh De'ah 2:69. Others also discuss the insertion of an instrument into the uterine cavity. Concern is expressed regarding bleeding due to the instrument itself coming into contact with blood vessels in the uterine lining. Cf. Darkhei Teshuvah, Yoreh De'ah 194:14; Beit Yitzhak, Yoreh De'ah 2:14.
77. Iggrot Moshe, Orah Haim, 3:100. Cf. Nishmat Avraham, Yoreh De'ah, 194:4.
78. Nishmat Avraham, Yoreh De'ah 187:2.
79. Quoted in Nishmat Avraham, Yoreh De'ah 187:2.
80. Hapardes (March 1961), 35:6, p. 33 as quoted in part by Rabbi Eider in Hilkhot Niddah. Cf. Kitzur Shulhan Arukh Hilkhot Niddah, chapter 4, sections 11-14 and footnote 13.
81. Kitzur Shulhan Arukh, Hilkhot Niddah, chapter 4, sections 11-14 and footnote 13.
82. Hymeneal bleeding caused by instrumentation, therefore, would be exempt simply because it is not uterine in origin. Only under normal circumstances of intercourse did the rabbis institute the restrictions of *niddah* for hymeneal bleeding, though it is not really uterine in origin. Otherwise, that fact is the operative one. It should be noted that the state of *niddah* that might be imposed with traumatic bleeding would probably only

be on a rabbinic level. This is due to the lack of the necessary sensation required to impose a Biblical state of *niddah* (see note 90). Regardless, the issue of traumatic vs. physiologic bleeding is probably the most fundamental one of significance for this chapter.

83. Resp. Iggrot Moshe, Orah Haim 3:100 and Yoreh De'ah 1:83. Cf. Havot Da'at on Shulhan Arukh, Yoreh De'ah 187:17 (in the Hiddushim) and 196:3 (in the Beurim), and Pithei Teshuvah on Yoreh De'ah.
84. Personal communication, Rabbi Hershel Schachter. Cf. Nishmat Avraham, Yoreh De'ah 187:8, subscript 5 for a lengthy discussion regarding the credibility of physicians.
85. Cf. *Current Obstetrics*, ed. Pernoll, pp. 615-616, 620-621,1030; H.W. Jones, III, A.C. Wentz, and L.S. Burnett, *Novak's Textbook of Gynecology*, 12th edition (1992), p. 266.
86. Darkhei Teshuvah on Shulhan Arukh, Yoreh De'ah 194:19; Kitzur Shulhan Arukh, Hilkhot Niddah, chapter 1, section 4. Cf. Nishmat Avraham, Yoreh De'ah 194:4.
87. Cf. Nishmat Avraham, Yoreh De'ah in preface to Hilkhot Niddah (p. 790.
88. Cf. Kitzur Shulhan Arukh Hilkhot Niddah, chapter 1, section 4, pp. 89-90.
89. Nishmat Avraham, Yoreh De'ah 194:4.
90. As previously discussed, while Rabbi Auerbach, Rabbi Waldenburg and Rabbi Karelitz all seem to claim that only natural and spontaneous physiologic bleeding creates *niddah*. Rabbi Pfoifer also adopts the exemption of *makkah* as the reason that Pap smears do not initiate *niddah* status. C.F. Kitzur Shulhan Arukh, Hilkhot Niddah, chapter 1, section 4. It should be noted that any state of *niddah* that could have been created by a

pelvic exam and Pap smear would likely have been on a rabbinic level. This would be due to the lack of the necessary sensation to impose a Biblical state of *niddah*. This point, however, is also open to dispute. Cf. Har Tzvi, Yoreh De'ah, No. 152.
91. Resp. Iggrot Moshe, Orah Hayim, 3:100.
92. Jones, Wentz, and Burntee, *Novak's Textbook*, pp. 283-284.
93. *Current Obstetrics* ed. Pernoll, pp. 900-901, 1030.
94. Ibid. pp. 618-619; Scott, Disaia, Hammond and Spellacy, *Danforth's Obstetrics and Gynecology*, 6th edition (1990), pp. 706-707.
95. Cf. Nishmat Avraham, Yoreh De'ah 194:2, subscript 4.
96. Shulhan Arukh, Yoreh De'ah 184:2.
97. Nishmat Avraham, Yoreh De'ah 194:2 subscript 2.
98. *Current Obstetrics*, ed. Pernoll, pp. 624, 1031; *Novak's Textbook*, pp. 291-292.
99. Ibid.
100. Personal Communication, Dr. Richard V. Grazi, Director of Reproductive Endocrinology and Infertility, Maimonides Medical Center, Brooklyn, New York.
101. Cf. Nishmat Avraham, Yoreh De'ah, 194:4.
102. *Current Obstetrics*, ed. Pernoll, pp. 1031-1032; *Novak's Textbook*, p. 293.
103. Ibid., *Current Obstetrics*, pp. 622-623, 1031-1032.
104. Kitzur Shulhan Arukh, Hilkhot Niddah, chapter 1, section 4 (p. 91).
105. Infertility should be considered in the category of *holeh she'ain bo sakana*, one who is ill but not dangerously so. This category includes one who cannot function normally, which is an accurate description of an infertile individual. For such a person, some rabbinic restrictions may be suspended.

106. Jones, Wentz, and Burnett, *Novak's Textbook*, pp. 268-269, 287; *Current Obstetrics* ed. Pernoll, p.1030
107. Resp. Tzitz Eliezer, XI, 38 and XII 44:5.
108. Resp. Iggrot Moshe, Orah Haim, 1:128; Shemirat Shabbat Kehilkhata, I, 40:2, subscripts 2, 3. Cf. Nishmat Avraham, Orah Haim, 306:7, subscript 2.
109. Shemirat Shabbat Kehilkhata, I, 40:3.
110. Shemirat Shabbat Kehilkhata, I, 33:20 and subscripts 81, 83; Nishmat Avraham, Orah Haim 318:11, subscript 2.
111. Shemirat Shabbat Kehilkhata, I, 33:20, subscripts 81, 83; and Resp. Tzitz Eliezer, X, 25:1.4 and 18:1.
112. Ibid. in Tzitz Eliezer, although Rabbi Waldenberg's specific line of reasoning is somewhat different than the one presented here. In fact, elsewhere he doesn't seem to consider an act such as the one involved in dipping the stick in urine as indirect. Cf. Resp. Tzitz Eliezer, XIV, 30 and 31. Regardless, he does, in practice, consider the color changes of a dipstick as being caused indirectly, albeit for a different reason than the one suggested here.
113. Shemirat Shabbat Kehilkhata, I, 33:20, subscript 83.
114. Shulhan Arukh, Orah Haim, 308:34,35; Mishna Berurah, subscripts 134, 136.
115. Ibid., Shulhan Arukh; Shemirat Shabbat Kehilkhata, I, 22:42.

III. THERAPEUTIC CONSIDERATIONS

INTRODUCTION

Although physicians commonly accept that female factors and male factors share almost equally in causing infertility, there is little question that the major focus in curing it is on the female. Several reasons may account for this. First, scientific understanding of reproductive physiology in women is more sophisticated than its parallel in men. As a set of biological phenomena, the mysteries and intricacies of cyclicity, conception, pregnancy and childbirth seem to have captivated scientific attention more deeply than the static and, to a certain extent, more simple system in the male. The result is that our understanding of the two is unequal. This is also interesting from a historical perspective, as it may stem in part from the time-honored focus on the woman as the exclusive cause of infertility. The reader should note that not until early in this century did physicians even entertain the thought that a sexually potent man may be infertile. In recent times, the development of a medical specialty dealing specifically with male infertility lagged far behind its counterpart in gynecology.

Another reason for focusing on the treatment of women may be due to their innate biology. That is, the cyclic system which characterizes normal female reproduction is exquisitely sensitive to stress. Not uncommonly, therefore, the experience of infertility and its accompanying stresses, regardless of the primary cause, will lead to physiological disturbances in the woman. Finally, and most obviously, it is the woman who must conceive. This means that many male disorders for which there are no direct cures (and, given our current state of ignorance about male reproduction, there are many) require procedures to be performed in the female. Together, these factors emphasize the centrality of the woman in most fertility therapies and the crucial role which her treating physician must play.

In dealing with a problem so emotionally charged and physically challenging as infertility, strong bonds are often formed between the affected woman and her physician that go beyond the typical doctor-patient relationship. Because of the unpredictable nature of certain treatments, the physician is continuously "on call" for the patient. Office visits may be required several times a week. Addressing the anxieties that accompany treatment, phone calls may come daily and at odd hours. In return for this level of involvement, the physician may expect that instructions will be followed unerringly. As the complexity of treatment grows, the commitment of each to its success is expected to grow accordingly. It is within that framework that the demands of halakha may be perceived as obstacles to success.

Sensitivity to the halakhically committed woman may require of the physician that he or she alter modes of practice. While attention to modesty in the office is always important, it suddenly becomes even more so. While repeated consultations with the husband may be routine, a fourth party — the rabbi — must now also be consulted. These changes in the style of practice that are made in order to accomodate halakhically committed couples may be perceived as intrusions which indirectly question the physician's competence or integrity. More importantly, the physician is given a new set of restrictions under which treatment must be designed. At times, those restrictions may actually *prevent* rather than promote pregnancy. It is exceedingly important, therefore, for the physician to understand and anticipate the needs of the Orthodox patient. Likewise, the patient must understand the limitations with which the physician must function. This chapter is written with these goals in mind. Building on the concepts developed in the previous section, it translates halakhic principles into practice. This is done, moreover, with the premise that the more physicians and patients understand the issues, the greater will be their respect for one another.

Finally, the interested rabbi or *posek* (rabbinic decisor) may also gain from the discussion which follows. Possibly, and with time, a newfound trust in physicians will also develop. This is sorely needed in these matters, where rabbinic doubts about the trustworthiness of physicians has fueled patient anxieties. And not without cause! The world is not a perfect place, and there are people who deal unscrupulously in all walks of life. Couples seeking treatment for infertility should indeed check the credentials of the treating physicians, and should have a sense of their ethical qualities. They should feel comfortable with both their level of professional expertise and the level of personal concern that accompanies their treatment. They should be able to discuss their religious concerns without feeling embarrassed or threatened. But, of course, this is important not only in the realm of artificial insemination, which has stirred so much controversy. This approach should govern the physician-patient relationship regardless of the type of therapy that is required. When a couple feels that their physician is on their side, and that he or she has in mind their religious values as well as their ultimate goal of having a child, they can comfortably trust that physician to do the right thing for them. Casting doubt on the motives of physicians in general does little but add stress to an already stressful situation. On the other hand, the couple who enters therapy with confidence will be emotionally prepared to persist in that therapy as long as it takes to achieve their desired goal.

THE PHYSIOLOGY OF CONCEPTION

Richard V. Grazi

The average person has a general understanding of "how babies are made." A somewhat more sophisticated knowledge of the reproductive process is necessary, however, for one wishing to appreciate the demands of fertility therapy on the couple and how they interface with halakhic concerns. While the language in the following short discussion is at times technical, the concepts are straightforward and easily absorbed. Figure 7 is a graphic representation of the events described below.

A. Sperm

Sperm cells are produced in the testes and carry half the genetic information necessary for the creation of a new human being. (The other half is contained in the egg.) This tightly packaged genetic material, consisting mostly of DNA, is protected within the sperm head. The tail, in turn, endows the sperm with motility, or movement, which is necessary for its delivery through the female genital tract and final

132   BE FRUITFUL AND MULTIPLY

union with the egg. Sperm are unique in this ability to propel themselves. Unlike eggs, which are produced in the ovary only during fetal life and never again, sperm are continually produced in large numbers during the reproductive life of every normal man.

Once ejacualted into the vaginal tract, sperm must undergo a long and complex journey before they are capable of fertilizing an egg. Most die in the vagina before they can traverse the cervical canal and enter the womb. Of the relatively few that do manage to survive, only a small number will actually be able to enter into the Fallopian tubes. Fewer still will swim successfullly to the end of the tube, where the

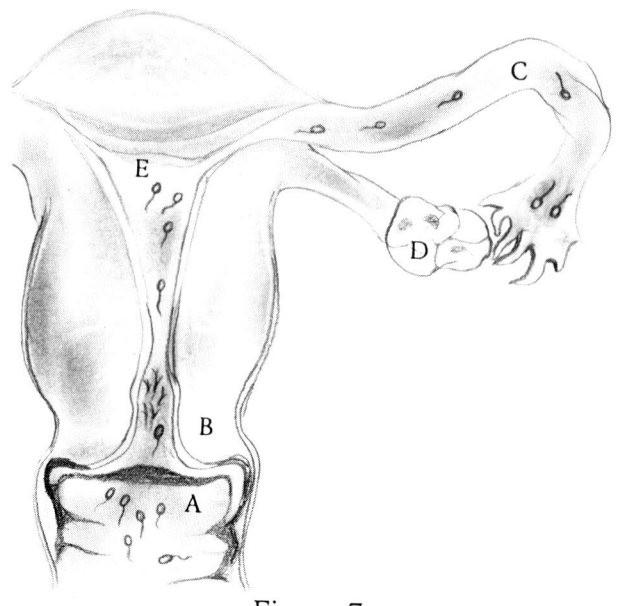

Figure 7.
How conception occurs.
Letters refer to explanations in text.

egg must be fertilized. Even then, the journey is incomplete. Once the egg is encountered, the sperm must be able to disperse the surrounding layers of cells, penetrate through the hardened shell of the egg, pierce the egg membrane and, finally, fuse with the genetic material contained in its nucleus. Because the process is so complex and, to a certain extent, inefficient, it is necessary that a certain critical number of normal sperm be present in the ejaculate to insure that at least one will successfully fertilize the egg.

Although it is difficult to predict with certainty the determinants of male fertility, most doctors accept certain criteria to define a male as fertile, subfertile or sterile. Mostly, these relate to the examination of sperm. In general, fertile males have greater than 20 million sperm in each milliliter of the ejaculate. At least 60% of those sperm must be motile, or moving, preferably in a straight and progressive way. Also, at least 60% must have normal morphology; or shape. Men with no sperm in the ejaculate (due to failed production or blocked ducts) are considered sterile. Sperm counts anywhere in between define a male as subfertile.

Clearly, measurements of sperm count, motility and morphology are not the only ways to assess male fertility. Currently, many different tests are being investigated as predictors of male fertility. Computer assisted semen analysis is being used to improve on the traditional technique. The sperm penetration assay ("hamster test") and the hemizona assay are being used to assess the fertilizing capacity of sperm. Biochemical testing of sperm is also being evaluated. Although all of these add to the time-honored semen analysis, none has proven to be entirely accurate in distinguishing male fertility from subfertility. Research in this area is active and ongoing.

B. Cervical mucus

After intercourse during which male orgasm and ejaculation has taken place, most women will sense that the seminal fluid "falls out" upon arising. This is normal and cannot be considered a cause of infertility. Indeed, the seminal fluid, which is the liquid medium in which sperm is delivered to the female, is always discharged after intercourse. Moreover, at almost all times of the cycle, the sperm within the semen is also expelled. There is only one interval during the menstrual cycle when this does not occur. This is at midcycle, during which time the mature egg sends a signal to the cervix (in the form of the hormone estrogen) to produce copious amounts of a watery substance called cervical mucus. Many women can determine their "fertile time" by the appearance of this watery mucus discharge, as it is a reliable sign that a fully ripened egg is about to be ovulated. The mucus acts as a reservoir for motile sperm, which penetrate into it upon contact. That is why, during the fertile time, even though the semen may be expelled, healthy sperm are retained within a woman's genital tract. There, sperm may live for up to 72 hours after intercourse. Only the most vigorous sperm can migrate past the cervix and into the upper reproductive tract.

Several conditions may render the cervical environment hostile to sperm. These include infections, antibody production and inadequate mucus production. The latter may be due to previous surgery or to abnormal hormonal stimulation. In any of these conditions, the cervix may act as a physical barrier to the progression of sperm through the reproductive tract, thereby impairing fertility. The impact of various fertility treatments on cervical mucus production will be discussed in the next chapter.

C. Fallopian tubes

After sperm traverse the cervix, they are propelled upward through the uterine cavity and through the Fallopian tubes toward the ovaries. But it is not enough for the tubes to simply be open; they are not merely conduits for sperm and eggs. In fact, they participate in the reproductive process in ways which, when disrupted, are difficult to overcome.

The inner channel of the tubes is lined by cilia, hair-like structures which help to propel the sperm towards the far end of the tube, where the egg is fertilized. Somewhat paradoxically, and in ways which are not completely understood, these same cilia propel the egg in the opposite direction, from the ovary toward the uterus. Using small, finger-like projections at its very end (fimbriae), the tube sweeps over the ovary and captures it within its inner lining. If motile sperm are present in this area, the egg will be fertilized. However, this too is not sufficient to initiate a normal pregnancy. The tubal muscle must undergo rhythmic contractions which, in concert with the motion of the cilia, bring the fertilized egg to the uterus, where it can implant. This process takes approximately three days, during which time the tubal secretions must be sufficient to maintain the enormous nutritional and energy requirements of the rapidly dividing embryo.

Unfortunately, the very specialized functions of the Fallopian tubes are exquisitely sensitive to even the smallest degrees of damage, in particular by infection. When blockage occurs, this of course results in sterility. But unblocking the tubes does not necessarily restore fertility. Although a variety of surgical procedures are used successfully to open blocked tubes, underlying damage to the propulsive and nutritional functions of the tube may still cause permanent infertility or, in some cases, tubal pregnancy. In the latter case, the fertilized embryo actually implants within the tubal wall. Because the tube cannot accomodate a growing fetus, however, the pregnancy cannot continue normally. This situation poses a grave hazard to the woman and the pregnancy (with or without the tube) must be removed.

D. Ovulation

Unlike sperm, which are continuously produced in vast numbers, the human ovary in general produces only one mature egg during each fertile cycle. Also, eggs have no innate propulsion system. As they are released through the capsule of the ovary, they rely on the Fallopian tube to transport them to proximity with sperm. Finally, egg production differs from sperm production in that it is a non-renewable process. The human female is born with all the eggs she will ever have, and 99% of them die before they even have a chance to be fertilized. Ovulation is the process by which an egg which has lain dormant — sometimes for three or four decades! — is activated, matured and released from the ovary.

Normal ovulation depends on a complex interplay between the developing egg and centers in the brain called the hypothalamus and pituitary gland. After puberty, the hypothalamus releases a hormone (gonadotropin releasing hormone, or GnRH) which is necessary for normal pituitary functioning. The pituitary gland, in turn, releases two hormones (follicle simulating hormone, or FSH, and luteinizing hormone, or LH) which stimulate growth, maturation and release of eggs within the ovary. The developing egg, mainly through its release of estrogen, interacts with the hypothalamus and pituitary in ways which control its own develpment and which insure that one egg is ovulated each month. After ovulation, the supporting cells of the egg become the corpus luteum (the so-called "ovulation cyst") and produce progesterone, which prepares the uterine lining for implantation of the fertilized egg. In the absence of pregnancy, the corpus luteum has a defined lifespan of 14 days. As it dies, hormonal production wanes and uterine bleeding follows. During this menstrual period, another egg is recruited for the following ovulation, a process which takes approximately 14 days. It is this continual replenishment of mature eggs and the limited functioning of the corpus luteum which is responsible for the 28 day, cyclic menstrual pattern of most women.

Because cyclic bleeding is the end result of a process that depends on the proper integration of so many hormonal signals, it is a phenomenon which can be disrupted at numerous points. Excessive physical stress, anxiety, undernutrition and obesity are among the more common conditions which can prevent ovulation and, therefore, cyclic menstruation. The so-called "fertility drugs" are all designed to manipulate the hypothalamus, pituitary and ovaries in order to stimulate ovulation.

E. Uterus

The goal of all reproductive processes is to produce a healthy, growing fetus within the uterus, or womb. Although anatomical obstructions within the uterus may occur, the more common problems relate to the uterine lining itself. This lining sheds and regenerates itself each month under the influence of hormonal stimuli from the ovary and its developing egg. Any disturbances in egg recruitment, development, ovulation, corpus luteum formation or hormonal secretion will translate into a disordered development of the uterine lining. In such situations, a fertilized embryo entering the uterine cavity is not likely to implant. If implantation does occur, the embryo is not likely to develop properly. Thus, a disordered uterine lining is commonly associated with infertility or repeated miscarriages. It should be noted, however, that this defect in the development of the uterine lining usually reflects a problem elsewhere in the hormonal system, and not primarily within the uterus itself.

F. Other factors

Listed above are only the main events in human reproduction. (A) Sperm need to be ejaculated into the vagina. (B) They need to penetrate into the cervical mucus and (C) they must find an open passageway to the egg. In addition, (D) an egg must be released from the ovary and, after fertilization, (E) it must be able to grow within a normal uterine environment. While these are all necesssary for conception, clearly they are not in themselves sufficient. Indeed, reproductive science is constantly shedding new light on the complexity of these processes. As our knowledge of genetics, immunology and molecular biology continues to increase, our sophistication with respect to reproductive physiology and the correction of infertility will also grow.

THERAPEUTIC SOLUTIONS

Richard V. Grazi

Artificial Insemination

Although in most instances artificial insemination is used in order to treat male infertility, a discussion of this procedure rightfully belongs in this chapter on treating infertility in the female. This is mainly because the procedure is performed on the woman, no matter where the problem lies. Also, in many instances, it is specifically used as therapy for female factors. Most important of all, however, artificial insemination is frequently used to overcome halakhic obstacles to fertility therapy. In subsequent sections, we will see how this procedure often arises as an option during therapy. But first, some definitions.

Artificial insemination refers to the placement of sperm in the female reproductive tract, usually the cervix, by means other than intercourse. The procedure is simple, requires few instruments, little training and, in fact, can even be done by the husband himself. It is meant to simulate what would otherwise happen during natural intercourse.

In the past, AIH (artificial insemination with

husband's sperm) was used to enhance fertility under in a variety of circumstances, in particular male subfertility. Unfortunately, it did not work very well. Today, AIH is rarely done. It is reserved for those rare cases when an anatomical (or psychological) obstruction to intercourse cannot be corrected.

The type of insemination most commonly used today is called intrauterine insemination, or IUI. Usually, IUI refers to the placement of the husband's sperm directly into the uterine cavity. It requires, first, that sperm be separated from the rest of the ejaculate. This is because semen contains substances called prostaglandins which, when in contact with the uterine muscle, may cause violent cramping. Also, seminal fluid is a potential source of infection. The procedure for separation of sperm cells from semen is called "sperm washing," and is usually performed in a laboratory under strictly sterile conditions. (Responsible laboratories maintain a variety of safeguards to make sure that semen samples cannot be switched.) After the sperm are isolated and concentrated in a small volume of a nutrient liquid, the suspension is injected into the uterus through a long catheter that traverses the cervical canal. This is not where most sperm end up after normal intercourse. It is believed that, by increasing the numbers of sperm that reach the upper reproductive tract, fertility may be enhanced. Although IUI is primarily used to treat male factor infertility, it is sometimes used to treat infertility that is unexplained. IUI is probably most successful when used to overcome a cervical barrier to infertility.

In vitro fertilization (IVF) involves the joining together of sperm and egg in a laboratory dish (hence the term "in vitro," which means "in a glass"). The fertilized egg, or embryo, which results is then transferred back to the uterus, where implantation and growth of the fetus must occur. Many changes and improvements have been made since the first successful IVF was performed in 1978. The most dramatic of these was the introduction of medications which stimulate the ovaries to produce multiple eggs, and the use of cryopreservation techniques in order to freeze some of the embryos for later use. Both of these developments enhance the overall success of each IVF procedure. We shall discuss new ethical issues raised by this procedure in a later chapter.

A further improvement of the original procedure was the development of a nonsurgical technique to remove eggs from the ovaries. As originally done, IVF required laparoscopy under general anesthesia. Today, almost all IVF is done using transvaginal ultrasound guidance. In this procedure, a thin probe is placed in the vagina which allows visualization of the ovaries and the eggs within them. A special needle is then inserted through the vaginal wall directly into the ovary and all visualized eggs are removed by suction. The procedure requires only mild sedation, and recovery is rapid.

Gamete IntraFallopian Transfer (GIFT) is similar to IVF except that after the eggs are removed, they are mixed with sperm and placed within the Fallopian tube via a laparoscopic procedure. Fertilization occurs naturally, within the tube. Future developments may allow GIFT to be done without laparoscopy.

Zygote IntraFallopian Transfer (ZIFT) is a combination of both IVF and GIFT. In this procedure, eggs are removed and fertilized as they are for IVF, but the fertilized eggs, or embryos, are transferred to the Fallopian tube instead of to the uterus. Both GIFT and ZIFT require that the recipient woman have at least one normal tube. IVF, GIFT and ZIFT are referred to collectively as Assisted Reproductive Technologies (ART). To a certain extent, all ART procedures require a form of artificial insemination.

Not all halakhic authorities allow artificial insemination, even though the husband's sperm is being used. Some authorities simply will not trust the physician to not substitute the semen of another man in order to guarantee the doctor's "success." Needless to say, a good personal relationship between the doctor and rabbi goes a long way in settling these concerns. Others regard sperm procurement for artificial insemination as purposeful, and it is therefore not considered *hash-hatat zera le'vatalah* (wasting of seed), despite the fact that sperm loss must be recognized as an inevitable consequence of all forms of insemination, whether natural or artificial. In general, most halakhic authorities are willing to allow artificial insemination with the husband's sperm if it is clear that no alternatives exist for overcoming the couple's infertility.

Several finer points warrant consideration here. For example, Jewish law proscribes conjugal relations during the *niddah* period.* Several authorities insist that insemination be confined to the non-*niddah* days of the wife's menstrual cycle; others do not. If in-

---

* The laws of *niddah* are discussed in full detail in a previous chapter (page 79).

semination must be done during the *niddah* period, the preference for obtaining semen by use of a condom during natural intercourse involves a new problem: the sperm must be frozen for later insemination. Medically, better results can usually be expected from fresh sperm; halakhically, there can be some objection to further manipulating the natural process. This dilemma highlights the importance of close and deliberate consultation between the rabbinic authority, the physician and the couple in treatment.

Some authorities hold that the child conceived through IVF has no halakhic relationship to the genetic father, as the conception takes place "unnaturally" outside of the wife's body. In that case, the husband could not fulfill the mitzvah of procreation through this procedure and there would be no reason to allow the semen to be procured. While most authorities seem to hold that the child conceived through IVF has the same relationship to its genetic father as it would had the conception occured naturally, some might prefer GIFT to overcome this reservation. If the insemination or IVF is done after the husband is deceased (using previously frozen sperm), the situation becomes even more problematic. Physicians should encourage their patients to consult with their halakhic authority on these matters.

Menstrual Cycle Disorders
I. Anovulation

The basic mechanisms involved in producing cyclic ovulation have already been described (page 136). Not uncommonly, these mechanisms break down. The result is that ovulation ceases (anovulation), or becomes irregular and unpredictable (oligo-ovulation). Disorders of ovulation are among the most common causes of infertility in the female. Fortunately, they are also among the most successfully corrected causes.

Depending on the cause of anovulation or oligo-ovulation, the physician may choose to use a variety of different ovulatory agents. These are discussed below, along with the halakhic considerations that must accompany treatment with each agent.

(A) Clomiphene (Clomid®/Serophene®)

Clomiphene is the most commonly used medication to induce ovulation. It is an anti-estrogen, which works mainly in the hypothalamus and pituitary gland to stimulte FSH and LH secretion. During the time that clomiphene is administered, levels of these hormones rise dramatically, stimulating egg development and maturation within the ovary. If this process is successfully completed, ovulation occurs and pregnancy may result.

Most women who are treated with clomiphene are anovulatory and therefore menstruate irregularly or not at all. To begin a treatment cycle, therefore, the period is usually induced (with progesterone or Provera®, a synthetic progesterone). Typically, a 50 mg tablet is taken orally begining on the fifth day of the menstrual period and continued through cycle day 9. Ovulation can be monitored in a variety of ways, including basal temperature charting, urine testing for the "LH surge" or ultrasound tracking of egg production in the ovaries.

When an halakhically committed woman requires clomiphene to ovulate, she should begin taking it later in the cycle than day 5. This will insure that her ovulation takes place after she has gone to the *mikveh* and normal marital relations are permitted. This is especially important in normal-weight or thin women, who may be very sensitive to the effects of clomiphene and in whom ovulation may occur rapidly. Because there is no natural ovarian cycle to contend with, delaying the start of clomiphene is ordinarily an easy thing to do. In fact, clomiphene can even be started after the *niddah* interval is completed, provided that the physician is assured that hormonal status has not changed by this time.

Two potential halakhic problems may arise during clomiphene treatment. The first relates to midcycle uterine bleeding, which can result from the anti-estrogen effects of clomiphene. When this occurs, it does not inherently interfere with the fertility-inducing effects of the medicaton. However, if as a result of such bleeding, intercourse becomes prohibited, the end result is the same. There are two ways to manage this problem. The first is artificial insemination with the husband's sperm (AIH). If rabbinic approval is forthcoming, this can be accomplished during the same cycle in which the problem is discovered. If such approval is not forthcoming, then that cycle will be wasted. This does not mean, however, that clomiphene treatment must be stopped. Often, the addition of small amounts of estrogen (e.g. Premarin® or Estraderm®) just after clomiphene has been completed, i.e. cycle days 9-14, will prevent midcycle bleeding. If it does not, adjusting the dose of clomiphene may do the trick. If all of these maneuvers are unsuccessful, clomiphene should be discontinued and different agents used.

The second problem with clomiphene also involves its anti-estrogen effects. Not uncommonly, women treated with clomiphene will have a seemingly perfect response, but will not conceive because the medication has interfered with their normal production of cervical mucus. This secretion, which is easily detected in cycling women and is a sign of impending ovulation, acts as a reservoir for sperm and as a conduit for their movement through the female reproductive tract. When absent or reduced, fetility is impaired. It is estimated that 40% of women treated with clomiphene will suffer from poor cervical mucus production. While estrogen treatment of the type described to overcome midcycle bleeding may sometimes overcome this problem as well, this is usually not the case. More commonly, insemination of sperm past the cervical canal (intrauterine insemination, or IUI) is necessary to overcome this clomiphene complication. Here, too, if rabbinic approval is given, IUI can be used effectively during the same cycle in which the mucus problem is detected.

(B) Pergonal®

Generically called human menopausal gonadotropins, Pergonal is presently available only under this trade name. Unlike clomiphene, which is a synthetic, estrogen-like compound, Pergonal is a natural hormone. Derived from the urine of postmenopausal women, Pergonal is a combination of the two pituitary hormones LH and FSH. These hormones are naturally found in both men and women, but postmenopausal women have an abundant amount. When concentrated as an injectable preparation, Pergonal is a potent stimulator of egg development in the ovaries (and, in some cases, of sperm production in the testes).

Because Pergonal does not have the anti-estrogenic side effects of clomiphene, many of the halakhic problems associated with those effects (e.g. midcycle spotting and decreased cervical mucus production) are not relevant to Pergonal therapy. Certain other problems may arise, however, and when they do they can be particularly distressing. This is because treatment with Pergonal is, by several orders of magnitude, more expensive, more physically demanding and more psychologically stressful than treatment with clomiphene. Aborting a cycle of treatment because of an unexpected halakhic problem may be devastating for the couple.

Tradionally, Pergonal has been used to induce ovulation in women who do not ovulate and who have failed to become pregnant with clomiphene. When used for this purpose, the concerns regarding early ovulation are similar to those discussed for clomiphene. If, as is standardly practiced, Pergonal injections are begun on the third day of an induced menstrual period, the rapid egg development which occurs may lead to ovulation before the *niddah* interval is completed. Therefore, it is best to begin therapy later in the cycle, around day 7. This virtually assures that the woman being treated will have been to the *mikveh* in time for her most fertile moment.

It may also be helpful for some women to completely delay Pergonal treatment until after going to the *mikveh*. This is because physical contact between the couple is restricted when the wife is a *niddah* and some rabbis will therefore not permit the husband to administer Pergonal injections. This strategy is only helpful, however, for women who do not ovulate on their own. If they do, and the goal of Pergonal treatment is to stimulate multiple egg production, therapy must begin as soon as possible after menstruation begins.

(C) Metrodin®

In the last few years, a new ovulatory agent has been used successfully to induce ovulation either alone or in combination with Pergonal. This medication, called Metrodin, is very similar to Pergonal and is administered with similar dosing schedules. The major difference between the two is that, unlike Pergonal, Metrodin contains only FSH (and no LH). Indications for using it vary. In all situations, however, those considerations which apply to Pergonal will also apply to Metrodin.

(D) GnRH

In certain cases of anovulation, where the cause resides in failure of the hypothalamus to secrete its hormone GnRH, this hormone may be replaced by either intravenous injection or injection just below the skin. Marketed under the trade names Factrel® and Lutrepulse®, this hormone needs to be administered through a special computerized pump which delivers a small dose every 60-90 minutes. The advantage of this type of hormonal therapy is that it very specifically replaces the missing hormone, it requires minimal monitoring and there are virtually no side effects. Because the therapy induces a normal menstrual cycle or one in which ovulation is slightly delayed, there are no specific halakhic problems relative to this therapy.

(E) Oophorotomy

In certain circumstances, a physician and patient may together decide that medications need to be avoided altogether. This is most likely to occur when anovulation is the result of a condition called Polycystic Ovary Syndrome. In this syndrome, egg development within the ovary never gets past its initial stages. As a result, multiple small follicles, or cysts, develop within the ovary. These cysts create a hormonal environment unfavorable for ovulation, and thereby exacerbate the condition. In recent years, several reports have indicated that by vaporizing those cysts with a laser beam directed through a laparoscope, normal ovulation may result for up to one year *without the use of medications*. This strategy needs to be remembered and used when the halakhic problems surrounding the medical induction of ovulation render such therapy overly cumbersome or frankly unfeasible.

II. Superovulation

In recent years, indications for giving clomiphene and Pergonal have expanded widely. There are now numerous situations in which women who cycle naturally are advised to take these medications. Often, the goal of therapy is to stimulate the ovaries to produce as many eggs as possible — an effect called "superovulation." These include: (1) Luteal phase defect, a condition where ovulation occurs but the hormonal output from the ovary is too weak to sustain a pregnancy. Generally, this condition is first treated with progesterone supplementation or clomiphene. However, certain women who do not respond successfully must then resort to therapy with Pergonal.

(2) Male factor, which can include a variety of conditions in which sperm production is inadequate to achieve pregnancy in the natural way. Usually, ovulatory agents are given and intrauterine insemination is performed in the same cycle, in order to maximize the numbers of both sperm and eggs meeting within the Fallopian tubes. (3) Ovarian adhesions, or scarring around the ovaries, which can prevent the tubes from bringing in the egg after its release from the ovary. If the tubes are normal and at least some portion of the ovaries are in contact with the them, superovulation may be tried in order to increase the likelihood that an egg will be released in the direction of the tubes. (4) Unexplained infertility, a most harrowing diagnosis but one which is given to about 10% of infertile couples. In this situation, where all diagnostic tests have failed to reveal the cause of infertility, clomiphene or Pergonal is often used empirically (that is, without the intention of treating a specific problem) in order to induce pregnancy. (5) Assisted reproduction, a global term for a variety of high technology procedures, the most well known of which are in vitro fertilization (IVF) and gamete intrafallopian transfer (GIFT). Almost all patients undergoing assisted reproduction have ovulatory cycles without medications but are given Pergonal in order to increase the number of eggs available for manipulation in the laboratory. It has been repeatedly demonstrated that the success of these procedures is directly dependent of the number of eggs harvested from the ovaries during a particular cycle.

One of the problems with clomiphene is that it may hasten an otherwise well-timed and normal ovulation. A woman undergoing treatment may, for example, change from ovulating on day 14 to ovulating on day 10 or 11, while she is still a *niddah*. One must be careful to anticipate this situation, and to plan accordingly. Of course, if artificial insemination prior to *mikveh* is permitted, and if sperm can be procured by masturbation, this alleviates the major concern. Even so, it is helpful to determine this before starting the cycle, so that last minute emergency rabbinical consultations — and the stresses they involve — are avoided.

Many women will not receive a rabbinic approval for early insemination. This does not necessarily rule out treatment with clomiphene, since some women will not experience any change in the timing of their ovulation, and will not require insemination. If ovulation is brought forward into the *niddah* interval and clomiphene therapy must for some reason be continued, it is best to delay the initiation of therapy until day 7 of the cycle, to allow the time of *mikveh* to approach as closely as possible. If this is done, however, it should be understood that delaying the start of clomiphene therapy most often results in the ovulation of only one egg, which may be contrary to the desired effect. Ultrasound monitoring of egg development would provide useful information in such cases.

Pergonal is almost always the drug of choice when superovulation is being performed in preparation for assisted reproducton. The halakhic problems accompanying the assisted reproductive technologies will be discussed separately. With regard to the use of Pergonal for *in vivo* fertilization in the otherwise cycling woman, the halakhic issues are similar to those regarding clomiphene and mainly relate to the frequent occurrence of ovulation prior to the completion of the *niddah* interval. Again, it must be stressed that the medical concept underlying this type of therapy is to maximize egg production. In order to accomplish this, Pergonal injections must be initiated as early in the cycle as possible; beyond about the third day, one egg will already have been selected to ovulate and no amount of Pergonal can induce others to mature. As the average length of Pergonal treatment is about seven days, it is not unusual for the Pergonal-stimulated ovary to be poised for ovulation on day 10. For the halakhically-committed woman so treated, the problem is obvious.

This problem is also an important one for the physician, and not only because the treatment may fail. In many Pergonal-treated women, estrogen levels rise dramatically higher than in the natural or clomiphene-stimulated cycle. If, at a certain point, ovulation does not occur, levels of estrogen will continue to rise and may pose a serious health hazard. This condition, known as ovarian hyperstimulation syndrome, may become severe and has been fatal in some women. It can be quite discomfitting for the physician to watch as his patient heads towards hyperstimulation, unable to let her ovulate because halakhic restrictions forbid intercourse for another day or two. This is a situation that no one wants to be in but which occurs with regularity. Again, anticipation of this problem and discussion of various solutions prior to commencing treatment are invaluable.

The ways in which the problem of early ovulation can be solved depend on each couple's specific halakhic position. As with the clomiphene-induced early ovulation, an acceptance of early artificial insemination with a semen specimen produced by masturbation allows for the most straightforward approach. Some authorities do not object to insemination prior to *mikveh*, but do not allow masturbation. If this is the case, a true Catch-22 situation results: insemination is allowed, but only if semen can be obtained through intercourse, and intercourse is not allowed. One possible solution is to have frozen semen from the husband available for use. This may be obtained by intercourse during any previous, non-treatment cycle (with the use of a special collection condom or *coitus interruptus*). If ovulation must take place prior to *mikveh*, the frozen sample can then be thawed and used for insemination. Not all authorities permit the freezing of semen for this purpose.

For couples who will not accept insemination prior to *mikveh*, or for couples who find themselves in the Catch-22 described above, therapy with Pergonal need not be completely avoided. One may embark on a treatment cycle, understanding that ovulation may occur at an inopportune time. Often this will not occur. If it does, having been prepared beforehand limits, to a certain degree, the emotional impact of the failed cycle.

Lupron®

Repeated early ovulation in the Pergonal-treated woman who cannot be inseminated presents a most frustrating dilemma to that woman and to her physician as well. By the time that the problem becomes obvious, both will have expended considerable energy in managing her treatment. As the fertile times will have been missed consistently, neither will know if the therapy had a chance of working. Still at square one, both will feel more stress than ever. Fortunately, a solution may be possible with the use of a second medication: Lupron.

In recent years, a new class of medication has been developed under the medical category called "gonadotropin releasing hormone analogs," or "GnRH analogs." Produced in a central area of the brain called the hypothalamus, GnRH is, reproductively speaking, the master hormone. It controls pituitary production and release of LH and FSH, which in turn control the ovary. GnRH analogs are produced by a minor modification of the natural GnRH hormone which allows them to selectively bind to the pituitary gland and exert the exact opposite effect, i.e. they *turn off* the secretion of LH and FSH. Without these two hormones, egg production in the ovary essentially shuts down. Estrogen levels, which are a reflection of egg production in the ovary, fall to basal levels and all menstrual cycling ceases.

Earlier, it was intimated that the woman who takes Pergonal is sometimes better off if she is anovulatory than if she cycles normally. Normal cycles mean that the complex interplay of internal hormones is fully functional. They also imply that egg production in the ovary is proceeding at the appropriate innate pace. Women who cycle respond less than optimally to Pergonal because the drug needs to override this operational setting. Pergonal meets no such environment in the woman who does not ovulate. When she uses it, the Pergonal is doing all the work. It's in total control. If ovulation needs to be delayed, it can be done reliably.

Pretreatment with a GnRH analog such as

Lupron is a means by which the cycling woman can be made to stop cycling and become more responsive to Pergonal. When the ovulatory system is interrupted, she becomes like any other woman who does not ordinarily ovulate; that is, she becomes more sensitive to Pergonal. As a result, ovulation timing with Pergonal can be controlled. With this strategy it is clear, therefore, that even a woman who cycles regularly can be given Pergonal and reliably be made to ovulate after *mikveh*.

The following example illustrates how this strategy works. In a woman who menstruates every 28 days, ovulation presumably occurs on day 14. One week later, on day 21, progesterone production from the ovulated egg reaches its peak. On that day, Lupron therapy should begin. The initial outpouring of hormones (FSH and LH) will not be perceived in the presence of high levels of progesterone. By the time the progesterone levels fall, towards the end of the cycle, Lupron's effect will already be established. When menstruation occurs, hormonal functioning in the ovaries will have been eliminated. In this scenario, Pergonal can be started at any day afterwards. Day 3, day 7, day 17 — each is the same as the next. (It is not recommended to start Pergonal too far beyond the *mikveh* time, however, because the effects of too little estrogen begin to be felt about then.) When Lupron is used in combination with Pergonal, there is virtually no Pergonal timing problem that cannot be solved.

Though a potent solution to Pergonal problems, the Lupron-Pergonal combination is not perfect. It was already mentioned that by the time menstruation occurs during Lupron therapy, the ovaries are functionally asleep. Because estrogen production is minimal, the lining of the uterus may not heal properly, and bleeding may be prolonged. If left alone, this continuous bleeding would negate the entire purpose of the Lupron. In this situation, therefore, one should add estrogens (either orally or by transdermal patch) to stop the bleeding. With estrogen treatment, bleeding ceases promptly. The estrogen should be continued during the first several days of Pergonal administration, until blood testing reveals estrogen levels to be adequate to sustain the uterine lining (>50 pg/ml). This is a process that can take up to a week to occur, but it occurs eventually in every cycling, Lupron-treated woman. With estrogens handy as a solution to Lupron-induced bleeding, the Lupron-Pergonal combination seems perfect.

III. Premenstrual Staining

Staining which repeatedly occurs a few days prior to menstration may result from a condition called luteal phase insufficiency. In this condition, the hormone progesterone is inadequately produced during the luteal, or second phase, of the cycle. This relative deficiency of progesterone results in poor development of the uterine lining and premature shedding. While not a particularly serious problem in most women, luteal phase insufficieney may be a cause of infertility. Infertile women who experience premenstrual staining should therefore be investigated for this condition.

The diagnosis of luteal phase insufficiency is generally made by endometrial biopsy just prior to menstruation. (Some doctors simply check progesterone levels at various intervals after ovulation, but this method of diagnosis is controversial.) If a luteal phase deficiency is suggested, a confirmatory biopsy during a subsequent cycle is usually recommended.

Not uncommonly, the biopsy results are normal and suggest that the premenstrual staining is not pathological. It may simply reflect the sensitivity of the uterine lining to falling levels of progesterone. In such women, the bleeding is a minor nuisance and does not need to be treated; but, even this minor amount of bleeding poses a halakhic problem because it renders the woman a *niddah*. For her, progesterone supplementation by vaginal suppository should be given just prior to the expected time of bleeding. It is then continued until the time that true menstruation begins.

When the diagnosis of luteal phase insufficiency is suggested, two forms of treatment are generally available. Progesterone supplementation may be given by vaginal suppositories (and sometimes by injection) just after ovulation occurs, and there are no halakhic consequences. Alternatively, ovulation induction with clomiphene may be performed. If the latter is chosen, attention should be paid to the concerns raised in the previous section on ovulation induction.

IV. Midcycle Bleeding

In a normal menstrual cycle, estrogen and progesterone are produced within the ovary by the corpus luteum after ovulation occurs. These hormones sustain the uterine lining and prepare it for pregnancy. When pregnancy occurs, hormonal signals sent by the developing embryo cause the ovary to maintain its production and release of estrogen and progesterone, a process which continues until the placenta is completely formed and able to take over. In the absence of pregnancy, on the other hand, these hormones are no longer produced. In response to the decline in estrogen and progesterone levels, the uterine lining loses its hormonal support and begins to break down. That breakdown is experienced as menstrual bleeding.

Even as menstrual bleeding occurs, the ovary is preparing itself for its next ovulation. Within its substance, one egg is emerging as dominant over the rest. As it grows, it produces increasing amounts of estrogen, which serves to repair the uterine lining and begin anew its preparation for pregnancy. It is estrogen from the developing egg, therefore, which is the major reparative hormone. When it is produced and released in normal amounts, menstrual bleeding is normal and self-limited. When it is deficient, menstrual beeding may be heavy and prolonged.

Deficient estrogen release and sustained menstrual bleeding are the hallmarks of the non-ovulatory cycle. Varying ways to induce ovulation in women who do not ovulate have already been discussed. But estrogen deficiency may also accompany ovulatory cycles. In particular, two types of estrogen deficiency are common, and both produce midcycle bleeding or staining.

Normally, at ovulation, release of the eggs and disruption of the surrounding cells cause estrogen levels to fall transiently. (Shortly afterward, those cells become the corpus luteum and begin to produce estrogen and progesterone efficiently.) In most women, there are no consequences of that brief withdrawl of estrogen. Some, however, are very sensitive to this and experience midcycle bleeding. Although this does not impair fertility in any way, this type of bleeding is an obstruction to conception in the Orthodox woman because it prevents her from having sexual relations during the most fertile time of her cycle. It causes "halakhic infertility."

Midcycle bleeding may also represent a truly pathologic process. The developing egg may not produce enough estrogen and, at midcycle, the normal decline in estrogen levels is therefore exaggerated. Under these conditions, progesterone production after ovulation will likely also be deficient. This "luteal phase insufficiency" is a known cause of infertility. It is especially important, therefore, for women who consistently bleed at midcycle to determine whether or not they have this problem. (For a discussion on diagnosing and treating luteal phase insufficiency, see section III.) Errors in diagnosis may lead to incorrect treatment and possibly to numerous religious obstructions to conception!

When no abnormalities are detected, it may be assumed that the midcycle bleeding is a result of the normal midcycle estrogen drop, and that fertility is otherwise normal. In such a case, attention need only be given to removing the halakhic barriers to conception. To do this, estrogens should be administered just prior to the time when bleeding usually commences and continued until after ovulation (usually days 9-16). It is important to use a low dose of estrogen, so that pituitary functioning is not altered. The dose may be adjusted upwards, however, if midcycle bleeding persists. Transdermal estrogen (e.g. Estraderm® 0.05mg) should be used because it delivers the natural estrogen (estradiol) at a continuous and steady rate. Cessation of midcycle bleeding is usually prompt and fertility easily restored.

V. Continuous Bleeding

On occasion, a woman may bleed every day, continuously and without interruption. The bleeding may change in intensity from day to day — she may even notice when actual menstruation is occurring — but it never completely subsides. As a result, she remains a perpetual *niddah*. Even when fertility is not desired, the resulting disruption in normal sexual functioning may cause profound marital stress. For the woman with this problem, aggressive attempts at correction are therefore urgent.

Under these circumstances, the most important factor to be ascertained is whether or not ovulation is occurring. Many high-tech methods for detecting ovulation are available, but the simplest and best for this problem is the basal body temperature chart. With this method, a woman records her temperature (taken orally, to within 0.1°F) every morning upon awakening. Over time, a pattern emerges which is easily recognizable and will suggest that ovulation either is or is not occurring. If it is not, or if there is some other evidence to suggest a disorder of ovulation, ovulation induction will usually reverse the bleeding and restore fertility. For those not wishing to conceive, estrogen/progesterone cycling — either with birth control pills or with cyclic estrogen and progesterone as given to menopausal women — will also safely reverse the bleeding but without restoring fertility.

The woman who bleeds continuously but who ovulates cyclically presents a different set of problems. Because the pattern cannot be explained by variations in estrogen and progesterone, other sources must be looked for. Certainly, a complete blood count should be checked and any anemia resulting from sustained bleeding should be corrected by dietary iron supplementation. At the same time, disorders of blood clotting, thyroid function and prolactin production should also be looked for. If normal, or if the physician is suspicious, endometrial biopsy should also be done. In this case, it is done not in order to look for a luteal phase insufficiency but in order to rule out uterine cancer. (Although uterine cancer is generally a disease of older women, it is sometimes seen in younger women, especially those who are significantly overweight.) If the biopsy is normal, uterine x-ray (hysterography) or hysteroscopy should be done to look at the internal uterine cavity. Often, a polyp or fibroid will be found; removing these will stop the bleeding.

If no source of the bleeding is found, the problem must still be corrected so that the couple may resume marital relations. Again, the method here depends on the goal of the couple. If fertility is desired, daily administration of a GnRH analog such as Lupron should first be given. This will cause all hormonal output from the ovaries to cease. The uterine lining will shrink almost totally, and bleeding will stop. After an interval sufficient to allow normal resumption of intercourse, Pergonal may then be added to induce a controlled ovulation. If used properly, bleeding will not recur unless there is no conception, in which case it is normal menstrual bleeding. The Lupron-Pergonal regimen should be repeated until pregnancy occurs. If pregnancy is not desired, birth control pills should first be tried. As a backup, Lupron may be given daily or once monthly in its depot form. After bleeding stops, it may be continued for up to six months. When the drug is finally withdrawn, normal cycling may resume and the bleeding problem may not recur. If it does, Lupron may again be used but, because of concern for its effect on bone content, estrogens and progesterone should be added cyclically. This so-called "add back" regimen may be continued indefinitely.

VI. Early Ovulation

Not uncommonly, a woman may find that she consistently ovulates before going to the *mikveh*. This is another form of "halakhic infertility" insofar as a nonobservant woman with a similar cycle would not suffer any impaired fertility. Of course, a most straightforward solution is simply to inseminate the woman artificially (using her husband's sperm) at the time that ovulation is detected, without regard to her *niddah* status. When there are no other obstructions to fertility, conception is virtually certain to occur. (This is an instance where a seldom used procedure takes on great importance for the halakhically-committed couple.) Rabbinic consultation is necessary before commencing this type of therapy.

Even when approval for this therapy is obtained, timing the insemination may present a technical problem. Generally speaking, inseminations are timed to the wife's ovulation. In order to detect ovulation most precisely, urine testing is done daily in order to detect the LH surge. Typically, inseminations are performed on the day following the surge and on the next day. This means that if the surge occurs on a Friday, a Saturday insemination would have to be scheduled. However, observant women will not be able to travel to the office on the Sabbath. In order to avoid this, LH testing on Friday should always be done as early as possible. If the surge is detected, and if the physician's schedule permits, insemination should be done on that day in order to have sperm available in the cervical mucus during the most fertile time. Insemination may then be repeated on Sunday, as would normally be done. Similar precautions should be taken in anticipation of any holiday where religious restrictions prohibit travelling to visit the doctor.

If there is objection, manipulation of the menstrual cycle in order to delay ovulation becomes necessary. Unfortunately, delaying ovulation in an otherwise normally cycling woman, while conceptually straightforward, is not always an easy thing to do. The pituitary gland, which ultimately controls egg development and ovulation, must be harnessed and manipulated in order to slow down the process. Commonly, clomiphene is used for this purpose. The experience with clomiphene, however, has been mixed. While successful in some women, it can actually *hasten* ovulation in others. Also, clomiphene has side effects, not all of which are easily detected. Among these are impaired development of the uterine lining and alterations in the secretion of cervical mucus, both of which by themselves may cause infertility. If clomiphene is chosen as first line therapy for early ovulation, therefore, two things must be checked. First, ovulation testing (BBT charting or LH testing) must be done to confirm that the medication is having the desired effect of delaying ovulation. Second, postcoital testing and endometrial sampling (biopsy of the uterine lining) should be done to insure that the medication is not creating yet another cause of infertility.

Because clomiphene is just as likely to hasten ovulation as to delay it, other types of therapy must also be considered. Estrogens, which suppress the pituitary gland's production of FSH (the hormone that makes eggs grow), can also suppress or delay ovulation. When given continuously, as in birth control pills, ovulation stops completely. If given very early in the menstrual cycle and for a limited period of time, estrogens will also affect the ovulatory process, but only enough to delay it a few days. For example, conjugated estrogens (the kind given to menopausal women) taken during day 2-6 of the cycle consistently delays ovulation. There is, however, a problem with this type of treatment as well. Not infrequently, because estrogens delay the whole process of egg development, bleeding develops when the estrogens are withdrawn, and it can be prolonged. So while ovulation may be successfully delayed, for example, from day 10 to day 15, the secondary bleeding that occurs delays the visit to the *mikveh* until day 17. If this happens, not much has really been accomplished.

A somewhat more complicated but very effective treatment combines the strengths of both clomiphene and estrogens. In this regimen, estrogens are given on days 2-6 of the cycle. On the last day, clomiphene is added and given through day 10, in order to stimulate egg development and thus prevent further bleeding. When this regimen is followed, it is important that monitoring of egg development by ultrasound be performed in order to detect precisely the day of ovulation. As already mentioned, postcoital testing and endometrial biopsy should also be done.

VII. Ovarian Failure

The spectrum of menstrual cycle disorders ranges from normal ovulatory cycling with minor bleeding disturbances on one end to complete ovarian failure and absent bleeding on the other. While ovarian failure, or menopause, may be considered a natural state in that all ovaries are eventually depleted of their egg supply, when this occurs before the age of 35 it is considered to be a pathological event. Moreover, no matter at what age it occurs, if fertility is still desired, the only alternative is using a donor egg. We shall discuss this question in a future chapter.

Anatomical Infertility
I. Tubal Infertility

Closure or malfunction of the Fallopian tubes may result from infection, endometriosis or previous pelvic surgery. When the tubes are open but surrounding scar tissue prevents them from working properly, simple laparoscopic surgery may be all that is needed to repair the damage. In more severe cases, as when complete blockage and extensive scarring exist, a more extensive laparoscopy or microsurgery may be required. In either case, Orthodox women should encounter no specific religious problems related to their treatment. Most surgical procedures are accompanied by bleeding that is uterine in origin. Although this may induce a state of *niddah*, the bleeding is usually limited and will almost always subside by the following menstrual period. With clear instructions from the operting surgeon, the couple may then resume attempts at conception in the natural manner. The same holds true for any type of reproductive surgery, no matter which part of the internal tract is involved. Tubal disease leads to halakhic problems only when surgery to treat it has failed. In such cases, only in vitro fertilization (IVF) can offer a couple hope for a biological child.

II. Uterine factors

Tubal damage accounts for the overwhelming majority of cases of anatomical infertility in women. Rarely, infertility may be a result of anatomical distortion or absence of the uterus, cervix or vagina. These cases are almost always congenital, meaning that they developed while the affected woman was still a fetus. Other than some minor defects involving the uterus (so called "fusion defects"), surgical correction is indicated. Depending on the severity of the defect, a fully functional reproductive tract may be achieved; alternatively, as with a congenital absence of the uterus and vagina, reproductive capacity cannot be achieved and surgical reconstruction is done mainly to allow normal sexual functioning. In such cases, providing that the woman has retained her ovarian function, a biological child may be produced with the use of in vitro fertilization and a gestational surrogate, in whom the embryo is implanted. Generally, surrogacy is not sanctioned by halakhic authorities. Gestational surrogacy is the only means by which a woman who has undergone hysterectomy may produce a biological child. Of course, this requires that the ovaries still be intact and functioning. (Many women are confused by the term "total hysterectomy." Medically speaking, this refers to the removal of the uterus and cervix only. Removal of the tubes and ovaries — called "bilateral salpingo-oophorectomy" — does not always accompany total hysterectomy in younger women.)

A final syndrome which affects the uterus and causes infertility is one which is a complication of dilatation and curettage (D & C), one of the most common surgical procedures performed on women. Called Asherman's Syndrome, this condition develops when the curettage, or scraping, of the uterine lining during surgery has been vigorous and has caused scarring. The scarred lining is incapable of responding to the ovarian hormones, which are otherwise normal. As a result, growth and shedding of the lining cannot occur and menstruation is absent. Modern surgical management includes the use of a thin fiberoptic telescope (hysteroscope) to cut away the scarred lining. Usually, this is followed by hormonal treatment designed to allow regrowth of a healthy lining. Provided that proper management of this condition is given, no particular halakhic concerns are evident. If treatment has failed, however, surrogacy may again be the only option for production of a biological child.

Endometriosis

Endometriosis is a condition in which the lining of the uterus implants and grows outside of its normal location, usually elsewhere in the pelvis. Retaining its sensitivity to the ovarian hormones estrogen and progesterone, it grows and bleeds with each monthly cycle. This process can cause severe pain, with or without scarrring of the tubes and ovaries. Doctors have believed for many years that endometriosis develops as a result of retrograde, or upstream, menstruation through the Fallopian tubes and into the pelvis. However, this phenomenon is known to occur in most young women, and clearly most do not develop endometriosis. Researchers now believe that the disease may reflect a breakdown in the body's immune system, but this is still only a theory. Endometriosis is also a perplexing disease, in that a woman having only minor degrees of endometriosis may suffer from severe pelvic pain, while another having the most severe form may experience no pain at all. In both, endometriosis can cause infertility. Eliminating endometriosis has therefore become a major focus of infertility specialists.

Endometriosis is usually treated with surgery, medication or a combination of both. As discussed in the section on tubal disease, there are no particular halakhic concerns regarding surgery in the pelvis. Although it may cause bleeding, the bleeding does not induce the *niddah* state and, in any case, usually resolves by the next menstrual cycle. With medical treatment, there are also no special issues. Although in the past a depot progesterone preparation was used, which caused prolonged and troublesome uterine bleeding, modern medical therapy relies on the prolonged administration of GnRH analogs. These are available as intranasal, subcutaneous or long-acting depot forms. The latter is probably the easiest to take. When given properly, a "medical menopause" develops. There is no egg production in the ovary, and there is also no uterine bleeding. As with the menopause, hot flashes are the most common side effect, and they can be annoying. Sometimes, the uterine lining becomes so atrophied that continuous light spotting occurs. This is enough to render a woman a *niddah*, and she may have this problem as long as the medication is given. If this occurs, a low dosage of estrogen, orally or by transdermal patch, should be given in order to repair the uterine lining and stop the bleeding. This amount of estrogen is not sufficient to stimulate regrowth of the endometriosis, and it may be continued for the duration of treatment with the GnRH analog. (A further benefit would be the disappearance of hot flashes.) If estrogen therapy is to be prolonged, however, one should discuss with one's physician the desirability of taking progesterone (Provera®) monthly or every other month, in order to allow the normal uterine lining to be shed periodically.

IV. New Ethical Issues

INTRODUCTION

The decision to engage in artificial procreation is a difficult one for any couple to make. The medical instructions and procedures that need to be followed are exhaustive, the time commitment involved is substantial and the process can be prohibitively expensive. Still, for many couples the greater difficulty is in coming to terms with having a child through a reproductive process that is distinctly separate from their intimate relationship. Indeed, they may need to work with an entire team of doctors, nurses and scientists in order to be successful. In the process, every detail of their reprodutive functioning is exposed. Far from being a natural outcome of a healthy, loving relationship, the baby they plan for will grow out of a calculated and precise clinical plan.

Within the halakhic community, there is no objection to harnessing scientific knowledge to improve the human condition. The biblical juxtaposition of the command "be fruitful and multiply" with "fill the earth and conquer it" suggests that man may intervene in and manipulate nature for the betterment of life. This consideration is the basis for the general halakhic acceptance of modern technology, including medical advances. In principle, therefore, the idea of procreating through the use of a medical procedure should be one that is acceptable to halakha. Nevertheless, the halakhically committed couple who looks to in vitro fertilization or any of the other assisted reproductive technologies must be concerned with the specifics of the procedure. That is, is there halakhic objection to any one of the steps required? A positive finding in this regard would render the procedure impermissable.

In the early days of assisted reproduction, when all that was available was in vitro fertilization using gametes from husband and wife, the issues were straightforward. Halakhic concerns were limited to methods for procuring sperm and eggs and of establishing parental identity. Although the latter concern led some noted halakhic authorities to disapprove of the procedure, many also allowed it. Today, the array of procedures that falls under the rubric of assisted reproduction has grown considerably, and so have the halakhic issues. In this section, we deal with some of those issues. While many (if not most) are still controversial and unsettled, the material that follows is meant to acquaint the reader with the bases for the ongoing halakhic discussion.

NEW ETHICAL ISSUES

Richard V. Grazi
and Joel B. Wolowelsky

Multifetal Pregnancy Reduction and Disposal of Untransplanted Embryos

We mentioned earlier that typical infertilty therapy involves stimulating superovulation so that the patient releases a large number of eggs. This in and of itself is not problematic, but it quickly brings us to two sensitive ethical issues: multifetal pregnancy reduction and disposal of untransplanted embryos.

If fertilization occurs through natural intercourse or artificial insemination, the mother-to-be may find herself carrying a large number of embryos — far more than can be carried to term. This creates a physical danger to both the mother and future children. The larger the number of embryos, the greater the likelihood that the pregnancy will terminate prematurely, leaving the babies in danger of physical and mental damage. If some of the embryos are killed — a harsh word, but used to understand the importance of the ethical problem — the survivors stand a better chance of surviving healthy and whole. If fertilization occurs in vitro, sucessful implantation often requires fertilizing many embryos, implanting a number of the healthy ones (not all will implant), and facing the problem of what to do with the "excess."

The Roman Catholic position on this is clear, straightforward and uncompromising. That is, "no moral distinction is considered between zygotes, pre-embryos, embryos or fetuses."[1] Reducing the number of fetuses is abortion and murder; destroying the untransplanted embryos is likewise condemned.

Abortion on demand is repulsive to the ethics of the halakha; however, within Jewish law, there are many situations in which a pregnancy may be terminated.[2] If the mother's life is in danger, each fetus is a *rodef*, an aggressor who may (or must) be killed to save the individual in danger. But if the danger is to the various fetuses and not to the mother, each fetus is an aggressor and victim with equal status; it therefore might not be permissible to put aside one soul for the sake of another.

The question of multifetal pregnancy reduction (MPR) was recently taken up by Rabbi Yitzhak Zilberstein in a responsum to the Israeli Medical-Halakha Group.[3] Searching for a legal analogy for this situation, Rabbi Zilberstein focuses on the case of a group of people who are in mortal danger and who can be saved by sacrificing one innocent member of the company. He notes that most halakhic authorities agree that in such cases all must allow themselves to die rather than themselves give up an innocent person. Yet, Rabbi Zilberstein finds a number of authorities who limit these rulings to cases where in theory the innocent person who would be sacrificed might have been able to escape.

If, however, it is absolutely certain that all would be lost unless one is forfeited, these authorities would allow some innocent people to be selected by lottery and sacrificed to save the others. (It is impossible to "select" the most viable or healthy of the embryos at this early stage of the pregnancy, and the selection is indeed a matter of chance.)

These conclusions apply to cases concerning full humans who have standing as viable persons. However, Rabbi Zilberstein continues, our case concerns fetuses, all of which are already condemned to death. MPR should therefore be allowed, he rules, noting that this might then be a case of "fetal lifesaving" rather than "fetal reduction." Rabbi Shlomo Zalman Auerbach, one of the leading contemporary rabbinic authorities in Jerusalem, is quoted elsewhere as also tending to allow the procedure in order to save the remaining fetuses.[4]

Rabbi Zilberstein's decision seems to assume that without MPR, none of the fetuses will survive the multiple pregnancy. This suggests that if the medical indication is that they would survive, albeit with serious physical and/or mental deficiencies, MPR might be ethically prohibited. Yet Rabbi Haim David Halevi, Chief Rabbi of Tel Aviv, also allows the procedure without presuming that all were otherwise doomed to death. He notes that there is no unanimity of opinion among halakhic authorities concerning abortion, with some taking a most restrictive position and others allowing abortion of Tay-Sachs fetuses in even the third trimester. As the vast majority hold that the abortion of nonviable fetuses is not at all homicide, he feels that because without reduction the fetuses will most probably be born prematurely and with serious physical and/or mental disabilities, a lenient position should be maintained. He therefore allows reducing the pregnancy to the extent necessary to insure that the remaining fetuses will be born healthy and whole.[5] Rabbi Mordecai Eliyahu, former Chief Rabbi of Israel, also allows the procedure, adding that the reduction could be done at any stage of the pregnancy, although it is better to do it as early as possible, preferably within the first forty days, the period for which halakhists take the most liberal position on abortion.[6]

Rabbis Zilberstein, Halevi and Eliyahu all maintain that the number of fetuses to be destroyed is a medical question that should be decided by the doctors involved, who must determine the minimum number which need to be killed to ensure a good prognosis for the mother and remaining fetuses. (Rabbi Auerbach is not quoted on the issue.) This puts an ethical burden on the medical professional to be completely current on the statistical and medical studies associated with multifetal pregnancy outcome and MPR, so that the absolute minimum number of fetuses to be killed can be reasonably determined. We use the word "killed" deliberately, because this is not an action to be taken lightly. Despite its clear moral permissibility, it leaves its mark on the family and should be thoroughly discussed before therapy begins. No halakhic authority suggests allowing MPR for convenience or choice, such as reducing twins to singletons.

Nontransplanted embryos fertilized artificially *in vitro* have no standing as fetuses in Jewish law. Rabbi Halevi rules that "all eggs fertilized *in vitro* have no standing as embryos...and one may discard them if they were not chosen for implantation, as the law of abortion applies only to [procedures in] the womb.... But *in vitro*, as was said, there is no prohibition at all."

A similar ruling is offered by Rabbi Eliyahu, who writes that "all fertilized eggs which are destined to be implanted in the mother's womb should not be destroyed, as a live fetus will yet develop from them. But those eggs which have not been chosen for implantation may be discarded." Neither authority offers any detailed analysis of his legal ruling, apparently considering the position to be obvious and noncontroversial from the perspective of Jewish law and ethics. Indeed, Rabbi J. David Bleich[7] has pointed out in his recent summary of halakhic attitudes towards fetal research that even an aborted fetus in the early stages of gestation does not require burial.

It is not unreasonable to assume that to some extent these rulings are based on the Talmudic statement that an embryo is "mere water" within the first forty days of conception and that it is not viable *in vitro*. If the embryo could be maintained artificially outside of the womb until much later stages of gestation, it is not clear if these rulings would apply.

Current medical practice is to freeze the excess embryos for future use, in case those implanted do not survive or another child is desired years later. Disposal of these embryos is a matter of current legal debate, despite the halakhic permissibility of disposing of them when it is clear that they will not be used. Again, the issue should be thoroughly explored with the couple before therapy begins.

These rulings have interesting implications for a number of other issues. Rabbi Bleich has noted that the tissue of a spontaneously aborted fetus may be used for research purposes if there is a reasonable basis for assuming that practical medical benefits will ensue within a reasonable time period (the specific details of which require individual analysis). One might well argue that untransplanted embryos, which never had viable status, might be used for the purposes of research before they are discarded.

One must keep in mind, though, that those rabbinic authorities who allow in vitro fertilization (IVF) do not consider the procurement of the sperm to be a "wasting of seed" because the procedure is used to overcome existing problems of infertility. It is not at all clear that rabbinic approval would be forthcoming for IVF solely for the purpose of research. Nevertheless, as Rabbi Bleich notes "Jewish law does not posit...an exclusionary rule that would, *post factum*, preclude the use of illicitly obtained tissue for an otherwise sanctioned purpose" such as medical research.

Genetic Screening and Sex Selection

The new reproductive technologies offer new opportunities for treating infertility, but they create, at the same time, new halakhic challenges and questions. Despite the fact that in vitro fertilization might be the only opportunity for conception, some halakhists are reluctant to approve the procedure, even if the husband's semen is used. The discussion here takes the view that IVF is permitted, at least if it is the only hope for having a child.

For some couples, the issue is not simply in having a child, but in having or not having a particular child. Sometimes, the concern seems frivolous to the outside observer, such as insuring the sex of the child or the color of his or her eyes. Sometimes the concern is significant to all, like avoiding the birth of a child afflicted with a debilitating or fatal genetic disease.

Until recently, this was basically an abortion issue. Amniocentesis could be performed during pregnancy and the specific genetic marker analyzed. Abortion would be the only alternative to avoiding the undesired birth. Chorionic villus sampling would allow diagnosis at an earlier stage in the pregnancy, and while early abortions are preferable to later ones, there is no blanket approval available. Of course, no halakhist would countenance aborting a fetus of unpreferred sex or eye color. Some, however, are willing to permit aborting a Tay-Sachs baby even relatively late in the pregnancy.

The new DNA amplification technology for IVF provides a new approach for consideration. It is now possible to identify the X or Y gene in an embryo soon after it has been fertilized in vitro.

In their landmark work on the subject, Handyside et al. indicated some of the ethical implications of this new technology. Some genetic disorders are X- or Y-linked.[8] Because the sex of the embryo can now be detected prior to implantation, it is possible to choose only embryos of a certain sex for implantation, guaranteeing that the embryo which develops is free of a specific sex-linked genetic disorder. Using specific gene probes, it is already possible to diagnose specific genetic disorders (as opposed to simply the sex) at an early stage. As the authors noted:

> The detection of inherited diseases in very early

preimplantation embryos would allow the selection and transfer of only healthy zygotes to the uterus. After preimplantation diagnosis, couples with a high risk of a genetically defective baby could embark on a pregnancy knowing it was free from a specific serious inherited disorder. These parents would avoid the dilemma posed by prenatal diagnosis later in gestation — whether or not to abort a much wanted but affected fetus.

We noted above that while halakha generally takes a conservative approach regarding abortions, many contemporary *poskim* (rabbinic decisors) maintain that untransplanted embryos have no standing and may be discarded. It would seem, therefore, that if IVF is used in order to overcome existing problems of infertility and if, in any event, only some of the fertilized eggs will be transplanted, then perhaps selecting one of a desired sex would be allowed.

Yet, one must keep in mind that those rabbinic authorities who allow IVF do so when IVF is used to overcome existing problems of infertility, as procreation is a religious obligation. It is not at all clear from the rabbinic authorities previously cited that IVF would be permitted for the sole purpose of sex selection, absent any existing difficulty in conceiving.

Similarly, screening untransplanted embryos for genetic defects probably would be permitted if IVF were done to deal with an infertility problem. However, permitting IVF solely for the purpose of genetic screening rather than overcoming a fertility problem does not necessarily follow. Therefore, further clarification about these issues by rabbinical authorities would be necessary.

Sex Selection through AIH

Rabbi J. David Bleich has noted that the Talmud offers specific advice on how to increase the probability of a male birth. With regard to sex selection, he concludes, the primary halakhic concern is not with regard to the decision to engage in sex selection but with the method to be employed.[9] Paul W. Zarutskie et al. conclude their summary of the clinical relevance of sex selection techniques with a note that "[s]cientific feasibility does not necessarily lead to desirability."[10] Neither does it necessarily lead to halakhic or ethical acceptability.

Rabbi Bleich has already indicated over a decade ago that, in his opinion, sex selection using AIH (artificial insemination with the husband's semen), after separation of the X- and Y-bearing sperm, would be prohibited. He wrote:

> The rationale upon which AIH is sanctioned [by halakha] is, however, predicated upon the consideration that such an undertaking is designed to fulfill the commandment, "be fruitful and multiply" and is not at all a form of "wasting" of seed. It must be remembered that in AIH procedures several ejaculations are combined for insemination. The entire ejaculate is deposited in the vagina and no portion of the semen is destroyed. Separation of androsperm from gynosperm is undertaken solely in order to enable insemination with one of the two, but not both. Thus the procedure, to be effective, must result in destruction of either the male-producing or the female-producing sperm. Hence, an attempt to determine sex in this manner

would be a violation of Jewish law.[9]

Rabbi Bleich's position seems to imply that if destroying part of the sperm were in and of itself sufficient reason to render a procedure halakhically prohibited, all IUI (and hence most AIH) procedures as well as all in vitro fertilizations would be unacceptable from the perspective of Jewish law and ethics. Yet current procedures continue to be approved by many rabbinic decisors in many different cases.

It is also not clear, if these standard procedures are permitted, why a procedure which further separates male and female sperm would be prohibited in preparation for IUI, as typically each fraction contains a sufficient number of sperm to effect fertilization *in vivo*. With regard to IVF, this further separation has no effect on the actual number of sperm introduced into the petri dish at the time of fertilization. Further, if those eggs fertilized in vitro which will not be transplanted may be discarded, it is not clear why sperm in excess of that required to fertilize the eggs *in vitro* cannot also be discarded. It would seem, then, that Rabbi Bleich's specific reason for rejecting this form of sex selection needs further clarification. This, however, is not to argue that the procedure is automatically permissible.

Sex Selection through IVF

The possibility of allowing IVF for the sole purpose of sex selection is summarily rejected by Rabbi Yigal B. Shafran, director of the Department of Halakhah and Medicine of the Jerusalem Religious Council: "With regard to life in general and reproductive issues in particular, our goal is not simply to realize one's desires, though they might be lofty, but first and foremost to continue as much as possible a natural [marital sex] life" and to minimize to the greatest reasonable extent the major halakhic difficulties associated with IVF.[11] The personal desire to have specifically a son or daughter, he maintains, does not override the halakhic imperative to maintain natural marital relations.

A similar position is maintained by Rabbi Yitzhak Zilberstein, who regularly contributes responsa to the Israeli Medical-Halakha Group. He notes that some halakhic authorities categorically forbid any form of IVF and that there have been halakhic questions raised regarding the genealogical status of the child, even if the husband's sperm is used. IVF is certainly an intrusion into the natural relationship between husband and wife, which Judaism considers to be imbued with holiness. "[Normally] God joins with a man and his wife [in creating a child]," he writes, "but here it is the doctor's hand [instead]." Given all this, he says, it is absurd to consider putting aside the general halakhic insistence on privacy in marital relations to allow one to bring into the world an infant which, according to some halakhic authorities, has doubtful halakhic status as the father's legal child, doubtful status as the legal heir, and whose only certain status is that of a male or female baby.[12]

Like Roman Catholicism, halakha considers natural marital procedures to be morally normative; in contrast to Roman Catholicism, it does not regard them to be morally absolute. Thus, abandoning the normative approach to procreation must be weighed against other moral imperatives. (In halakhic Judaism, this judgment is relegated to the rabbinic authorities, not to the individual conscience.) Accordingly, the religious obligation to procreate can sometimes outweigh the imperative to maintain natural procedures and AIH or IVF might be allowed to overcome a fertility problem. Indeed, we note that it is most poignant that the Biblical command (Genesis 1:28) to "be fruitful and multiply" is coupled with the charge "to fill the earth and subdue it." This latter duty, explains the late Rabbi Joseph B. Soloveitchick, one of the major contemporary halakhic authorities, empowers and obligates man to attempt to gain scientific domination and control over nature, provided, however, that it is done with a sense of moral responsibility.[13]

But despite the willingness of halakhic authorities to allow artificial reproductive techniques to overcome an infertility problem, Rabbis Shafran and Zilberstein regard the rabbinic judgment to be that securing a baby of a desired sex is simply too frivolous a halakhic concern — no matter how pressing it might be for the specific couple — to overcome the other moral objections. Presumably, this would extend to preimplantation screening for other genetically controlled physical attributes, such as the color of the infant's eyes. (But, as we observed earlier, it would seem that if IVF is used in order to overcome existing problems of infertility and if, in any event, only some of the fertilized eggs will be transplanted, then selecting ones with a desired physical characteristic might be allowed. Further halakhic clarification is needed on this point.) The *Instruction* considers IVF to be morally absolutely illicit in and of itself; other considerations, such as the desire to conceive a baby of a particular sex or with a specific physical characteristic, certainly become irrelevant.

Genetic Screening through IVF

Rabbi Zilberstein's position on sex selection through IVF notwithstanding, he further rules that "one cannot close the door in the face of despondent people who suffer mental anguish in fear of giving birth to sick children, pressure which can drive the mother mad. Therefore, in the case of a serious genetic disease which affects the couple, it is difficult to forbid the suggestion [for genetic screening through IVF]."[12]

This permissive attitude towards screening and, implicitly, the discarding of the affected untransplanted embryos rests to a great extent on the lack of standing the embryo has in halakha. However, it is the psychological state of the parents which is invoked rather than any negative quality of life that the child might suffer.

In the case of genetic screening, Rabbi Zilberstein holds that the objections to IVF give way in the face of more pressing considerations. The artificial reproductive techniques are viewed, in a sense, as a therapeutic procedure for the parents. This does not allow for the indiscriminate relaxation of all associated halakhic prohibitions. Balancing the halakhic counterclaims in such circumstances is the duty of the rabbinic decisor addressing a particular individual case, not the privilege for the couple concerned. It might be reasonable to suggest that in an individual case where selecting the sex of the fetus was a serious and not a frivolous consideration, Rabbis Zilberstein and Shafran might consider an individual dispensation from their rulings prohibiting sex selection through IVF. Again, this is a question which would require further rabbinic clarification.

IVF vs. Uterine Lavage

Rabbi Shafran[11] too notes the need to address sympathetically the problem of genetic testing, but suggests that a uterine lavage (UL) be used instead of IVF. UL involves flushing out the embryo soon after it has been fertilized *in vivo* through natural marital relations. John E. Buster compared the advantages and disadvantages of embryo transfer as obtained through UL or IVF.[14] (Buster considered cases of UL from a donor. This generated issues that do not concern our case, in which the embryo will be transferred back to the genetic mother after screening.) One of his major considerations was that UL is a nonsurgical procedure that can be performed in an office setting without anesthesia, while IVF is an invasive procedure requiring anesthesia and laparoscopy with full operating room support. This consideration has been rendered obsolete with the acceptance of transvaginal ultrasound-guided follicular aspiration as the standard procedure for IVF. This procedure is minimally invasive and requires only mild sedation.

There are other considerations which make IVF a more practical solution than UL. IVF following gonadotropin stimulation of the ovaries inevitably yields a higher number of embryos than does UL, since ova may be harvested from ovarian follicles that would not normally ovulate *in vivo*. The IVF procedure also reduces the risk of ovarian hyperstimulation. With UL, there is a risk of an incomplete flush which could result in an unscreened pregnancy. (Marc V. Sauer et al. discussed post-lavage administration of high-dose contraceptive pills, endometrial aspiration or RU 486 following superovulation.[15] But this would be contraindicated if the embryo is to be transferred back to the genetic mother.) The risk of ectopic pregnancy may also be increased by UL.

There are two halakhic considerations that must be considered. UL involves a procedure that is at least closely related to abortion. IVF involves a more dramatic interruption of natural marital relations and the necessity for birth control to avoid natural conception without screening.

Rabbi Shafran concedes that UL brings us close to the issue of abortion within the first forty days of conception. While halakhists take the most liberal position on abortion during this period, there is no blanket approval for such abortions. Nevertheless, he feels that the procedure should be allowed because (1) there is a serious, significant, and legitimate need; (2) the lavage takes place before the embryo has implanted; (3) if the embryo is returned for implantation, no abortion will have occurred; (4) if the embryo has a serious genetic defect, it might not be viable and therefore need not be returned.

Indeed, Rabbi Shafran feels that any reservations about the procedure fall in the face of the halakhic obligation to minimize as much as possible any interference with normal marital relations. "There is justification to examine an individual case [to allow genetic screening through IVF] only if a uterine lavage cannot be used and we are dealing with a serious fear of a genetic defect," he concludes. However, in a subsequent clarification,[16] Shafran indicated that if current medical practice demonstrated that IVF were indeed safer for the mother and potential fetus, he would reconsider his position.

Halakhic Judaism considers natural marital procedures to be morally normative; but it does not regard them to be morally absolute. Thus, halakhah in principle has no objection to new in vitro technology, despite the fact that it might create additional opportunities for substituting artificial fertilization for natural conception. Indeed, it sees in the new technology an opportunity for alleviating pain and suffering, but one not to be used for what it considers to be frivolous considerations. It reserves for rabbinic authorities and not the couple itself the right to decide which situations allow for artificial intervention and which do not. These decisions may change over time as a result of collegial rabbinic interaction, changing medical technology, or — in specific individual cases — the psychological condition of the individuals concerned.

Donor Gametes

There are some physiological conditions which simply cannot be corrected by the new reproductive technologies. Foremost among them is the case where a man cannot produce sperm or a woman has no eggs to be released from her ovaries. In such a case, the only possibility of effecting a pregnancy is to use donor gametes (sex cells) in place of those which would have been supplied from the sterile spouse. In the case of donor sperm, the procedure is simple, involving very little technology. In the case of donor eggs, the technology is much more complicated, but well within the parameters of basic infertility technology. However, in both cases the ethical issues are complex and involved.

Even the Ethics Committee of the American Fertility Society could not reach unanimous agreement on the ethics of donor gametes. Five major objections were noted in the minority dissent: (1) The procedure severs procreation from the marital union, violating the exclusive nature of the marriage covenant. (2) It brings into the world a child with no bond of origin and therefore blurs the child's genealogy and potentially compromises the child's self-identity. (3) It encourages adultery by creating an environment wherein insemination of a wife by the sperm of another man is considered morally acceptable. (4) It marks a subtle but unmistakable move toward eugenics. (5) It tends to absolutize sterility as a disvalue and childbearing as a value, thus distorting and threatening the value of marriage and family. Virtually all halakhists — including those who are willing to allow donor gametes under certain conditions — share these reservations.

Adultery

The two ends of the halakhic spectrum regarding adultery as a component of AID (artificial insemination with donor sperm) are defined by the respective opinions of Rabbi Yoel Teitelbaum[17] and Rabbi Moshe Feinstein,[18] two of the most prominent late American rabbinic authorities of modern times . Rabbi Teitelbaum (known popularly as the Satmer Rebbe) argues that the halakhic definition of adultery is the deliberate introduction of a third party's semen into the vagina of a married woman. He therefore condemns heterologous insemination as morally repugnant and concludes that a wife who undergoes such a procedure is an adulteress. The concurrence of the husband is no more relevant than it would be in the case of sexual relations between a married woman and a man not her husband. Following through on the logic of his definition, he argues that the person who mechanically introduces the semen is also guilty of adultery.

There is some indication that this perception is maintained even by many of those couples who have opted for the procedure. For example, Klock and Maier[19] reported that while 69% of the surveyed couples who had undergone AID expressed no preference about the gender of the person performing the insemination, of those 31% with a preference, all preferred a female inseminator. One of the explanations they offer for this phenomenon is that "both men and women may prefer a female doing the insemination to decrease the connotations of another man and adultery."

(Interestingly, under this rubric, one might argue that in vitro fertilization could escape any censure of adultery, as it is a human embryo and not a man's semen which is being introduced. Donor insemination of eggs is a relatively new phenomenon and has received much less halakhic analysis. Charges of adultery have not been leveled against egg donors.)

Rabbi Teitelbaum's position is summarily rejected by Rabbi Feinstein. Rabbinic authorities cite two sources in refuting the charge of adultery. The first is the case of Ben Sira, the grandson of Jeremiah the Prophet, whose daughter, according to tradition, was impregnated by her father's semen while bathing in a pool into which her father had previously ejaculated. Ben Sira is considered legitimate. The second is a ruling by the medievalist Rabbi Peretz ben Elijah of Corbeil which sets out what has become the dominant current rabbinic view:

> A woman may lie on her husband's sheets but should be careful not to lie on sheets upon which another man slept lest she become impregnated from his sperm....Since there is no forbidden intercourse, the child is completely legitimate even from the sperm of another....However, we are concerned about the sperm of another man because the child may [unknowingly] eventually marry his [half-] sister.

Rabbi Feinstein would not give *carte blanche* approval to donor insemination, as we shall soon discuss. But he nonetheless argues from this source that adultery is not the basis of the concern that a woman be impregnated accidentally. In his view, physical sexual contact is part of the definition of adultery, and absent such contact the wife cannot be charged with promiscuity (nor can the child be branded illegitimate). He cautions, however, that the fidelity required in marriage commands that donor insemination is prohibited without the husband's consent.

Others, however, have argued that even if the charge of adultery cannot be sustained, the source's ruling cannot be extended to permit donor insemination. A woman may not lie on the sheets upon which another man slept despite the far-fetched and unintended possibility that she be impregnated; *a fortiori* she may not allow insemination by a person other than her husband even if she cannot technically be charged with adultery. Rabbi Eliezer Yehuda Waldenberg,[20] a member of Israel's High Rabbinic Court, argues that even if technical halakhic objections cannot be marshaled to oppose AID, the procedure runs counter to basic halakhic values which stress genealogy and family integrity. He cautions that whether or not the charge of adultery is technically sustainable, AID without the husband's consent is grounds for divorce.

Donor Gametes as Therapy

The Ethics Committee had noted (without explanation) that it consciously used the term AID instead of TID (therapeutic insemination — donor) in its report. Indeed, it is not clear to what extent the procedure itself can be considered therapeutic within halakha.

Donor insemination is not curative in that it does not overcome the husband's inability to impregnate his wife. The wife is not suffering from any physical ailment; rather, she and her husband are frustrated in the desire for her to deliver a child. Fulfillment of a person's desire is not, in and of itself, properly designated as therapy, especially if it involves otherwise objectionable means. For example, most people would hesitate to call adultery therapeutic if it were the medium adopted to overcome the husband's infertility, even if it were carried out with the husband's consent (and called NID: natural insemination — donor). Thus, Rabbi Yitzhak Yaakov Weis[21] condemns AID for nothing more than the "promiscuous" activity wherein the woman lies unclothed before the physician who, in turn, manipulates her reproductive organs simply to satisfy her desires. Use of the term TID would mask, to some extent, the moral and ethical problems associated with AID.

The above notwithstanding, the psychological state of the people involved is a legitimate halakhic consideration, and it may in some cases be weighed against the more general halakhic values. As Rabbi Aharon Lichtenstein noted:

> A sensitive *posek* recognizes both the gravity of the personal circumstances and the seriousness of the halakhic factors....He might stretch the halakhic limits of leniency where serious domestic tragedy looms, or hold firm to the strict interpretation of the law when, as he reads the situation, the pressure for leniency stems from frivolous attitudes and reflects a debased moral compass.[22]

While Rabbi Feinstein was adamant in his position that heterologous insemination (from a non-Jewish donor) violated no technical halakha, he was equally resolute in his position that such a procedure was only a course of last resort. He was careful to caution that he would permit the procedure only in the extreme instance where the wife is under severe mental stress and the individual circumstances have been reviewed by a competent halakhic authority. There is no promiscuity involved, he ruled, as there is no such intent or sexual arousal. AID, otherwise ethically questionable as a general procedure, might be allowed as therapy for a distraught woman suffering psychologically from her husband's infertility, there being no technical problem of adultery or possible future incest. But it becomes acceptable only when she (and her husband) cannot be reconciled to either a childless marriage or adoption. He does not address the question of egg donations directly. It seems logical to presume that a similar position would apply to that procedure. However, there might be several other technical halakhic issues, similar in some respects to the problems raised by the host mother and surrogate mother issues, which would have to be considered. We discuss some of these problems below.

Of course, this assumes that donor gamete procedures will actually heal the woman and not do harm to the family. Halakhists opposed to donor insemination despite the fact that it may not violate technical prohibitions often maintain that, in the final analysis, the procedure will lead to divisiveness, jealousy on the part of the husband, mental anguish, and so on. (There would be less fear of this in the case of egg donation, where both the husband and wife are the halakhic parents.) For these reasons, even Rabbi Feinstein warns that donor insemination should be discouraged. Certainly a couple considering the procedure must undergo serious counseling beforehand to insure to the greatest extent possible that the donor gamete procedure will have a therapeutic rather than damaging effect on the family. This is a decision that cannot be undone and shoud not be taken lightly.

Paternity and Maternity Issues

Halakha works on two levels. On the first, it must deal with the question of whether or not to allow a procedure. On the second, it must confront the consequences of a procedure already done. In general, while Rabbi Feinstein's lenient position on allowing donor insemination in limited circumstances has not been received enthusiastically, his ruling that charges of adultery (against the wife) and illegitimacy (against the child) cannot be sustained has emerged as dominant.

But there are other issues that must be confronted once donor gamete therapy has been effected. For example, secular law may hold that the husband who consents to his wife's insemination by a donor is the legal father of the resulting child. But halakha knows of no legal procedure by which a genetically unrelated person can be considered the full legal father of a child. By virtue of his consent, the sperm recipient's husband (like an adopting father) might have assumed those legal obligations to support and educate the child that usually evolve only on the natural parent. However, when the husband dies, he is assumed to be halakhically childless with regard to inheritance and other religious issues.

If the child inherits on the basis of the false assumption that he or she is the legal heir of the husband, the true legal heirs have in effect been robbed of their righteous inheritance. This problem be easily resolved by preparing a proper will. If the husband has brothers, his widow, like any childless widow, would have to participate in a special religious ceremony *(halizah)* before she could remarry. (No ceremony is required if the deceased had no brothers.) If the donor insemination were kept secret, the widow might not want to disclose the fact after her husband's death and would marry without the ceremony in violation of Jewish law. Fear of creating such a situation is quoted by opponents of donor insemination. Rabbi Feinstein dismisses this as a false concern, arguing that there is no reason to conclude that the widow would violate halakha to maintain the secret. Couples sensitive to halakhic values should be made aware of these issues in the physician's counseling session.

The situation is further complicated if the husband is a Kohen (descendant of the priestly class) or a Levi (descendant of the levites). Such status is inherited from the father and obviously the husband's status does not evolve on a child fathered through artificial insemination. Rabbi Shlomo Zalman Auerbach[23] maintains that in the case of insemination from a non-Jewish donor, the child takes on the status of the mother, becoming a Kohen or Levi if his maternal grandfather has that status. The social problems arising from a situation where the father is a Kohen and his son is not should be thoroughly explored with the couple before donor insemination.

Halakha does recognize paradigms in which the genetic reality is considered irrelevant. For example, halakha rules that conversion involves such a personal transformation that all previous genetic bonds are severed and, therefore, a brother and sister who convert to Judaism could theoretically marry each other, as their sibling relationship no longer exists. (This was forbidden rabbinically as it violated the sense of public propriety.)

Rabbi J. David Bleich[24] recently summarized the halakhic discussion as it relates to artificial reproduction. Some halakhists maintain that it is the physical acts of intercourse and birth that establish

New Ethical Issues

the legal bonds of parenthood, and therefore the genetic father of a child conceived through artificial insemination has no legal relationship to the child, even if he is the legal husband of the mother. However, the majority consensus is that whether fertilization is achieved through artificial insemination or in vitro fertilization, the genetic father maintains the same relationship to the child as if the insemination had been accomplished through natural intercourse.

The issue is more complicated with regard to egg donation. Rabbi Bleich concludes that while there is general agreement that the birth mother is to be regarded as the halakhic mother, one cannot yet dismiss the possibility that the genetic mother might *also* have to be considered the mother (thereby giving the child two halakhic mothers). If the donor and birth mother are not of the same religion, there is debate on the religious identity of the child. (The religion of the father is immaterial, as halakhic religious identity is determined only by the mother.) For these and related reasons, a fertile woman undergoing therapy that involves retrieving eggs for in vitro fertilization might not be able to comply with the demands of some centers that "excess" eggs be made available for anonymous donation to an infertile woman, especially if she is not Jewish.

Because *halakha* places great emphasis on establishing paternity, it requires that a divorced or widowed woman wait three months before remarrying (so that the father of a future child not be in doubt). Such a period of sexual abstinence, before and after donor insemination, might be required, especially if a testicular biopsy showed that a husband with zero sperm count had some sperm.

Fear of possible future incest

A serious halakhic objection to allowing anonymous donor gamete procedures would be creating and encouraging a system that might allow half-siblings who unknowingly share a common genetic parent to marry. In American civil law — which relegates to itself the ability to sever genetically created familial relationships — these unions would not be improper. But that is not the case for the halakhic system.

Jewish law posits a dual legal structure. It asserts a universal human morality, which it sees as binding on all people, and a specifically Jewish system, which is generally more stringent but which is applicable only to Jews. A sexual relationship between paternal half-siblings all of whose parents are Jewish is considered halakhically incestuous. However, in contrast to most contemporary secular societies, halakha sees no incestuous relationship between half-siblings who have a common non-Jewish father (irrespective of the religion of the mothers). On the other hand, a relationship between half-siblings who have a common mother (Jewish or not) would be incestuous irrespective of the religion of the fathers.

The logical conclusion of this position is that no fear of future incest would exist if a Jewish women is inseminated by the semen of a non-Jew. In such cases, the child has no halakhic father and hence no halakhic sibling relationship with any of his other progeny. However, if the donor is Jewish, he is the child's halakhic father.

For this reason, a Jewish couple who is sensitive to halakhic concerns should insist on obtaining donor semen from a non-Jew. The child is fully

Jewish (because the mother is) and, because he or she has no halakhic relationship to the donor, there is no danger of possible future incest. Not all couples are aware of this, and the physician should bring up in his or her counseling session the fact that, halakhically, it is preferable to choose a non-Jew as the sperm donor.

All halakhists prohibit a Jewish man from donating sperm to inseminate a woman other than his wife. There is a general reluctance to allow egg donation based on the unsettled questions of religion and maternity (including the problem of future incest), the prohibition for the husband to masturbate to provide semen for the in vitro fertilization, and the pervading distaste for violating the exclusive nature of the marriage relationship.

Intrafamiliar Gamete Donations

Incest and adultery share common public censure. It is therefore interesting to note a report by Robertson[25] that the Voluntary Licensing Authority in the United Kingdom will not license an IVF clinic that accepts the recipient's sister as an oocyte (egg) donor and that Victoria, New South Wales, and South Australia also ban such donations. Robertson is of the opinion that in the United States a legal ban on intrafamiliar gamete donations would raise serious constitutional problems.

It is also interesting to note the report by Sauer et al.[26] that although similar in concept, disparity exists regarding the use of male or female siblings for gamete donation. Most ovum transfer patients surveyed had not only considered using a sister, but 61% had secured such an agreement. On the contrary, only 11% of the couples undergoing AID would agree to using a brother as their donor, and none had actually asked one to participate. The authors do not suggest a reason for this disparity; perhaps an explanation lies in the fact that sperm donation requires sexual arousal, while egg donation is clearly clinical and devoid of any sexual element.

It is the legal bonds of marriage that underlie a possibility of adultery; legally severing those bonds would make the relationship ethically and legally permissible. Incest, however, is determined by the natural (as opposed to legal) relationship between the individuals. Thus Rabbi Yigal Shafran[27] is of the opinion that donor gametes might be permissible if technical arguments obviated the problem of adultery. However, no legal technical argument could be used to justify donor gametes if it involves a relationship which would have been incestuous if carried out naturally.

Because egg donation is a complicated procedure involving, at the least, discomfort and inconvenience for the donor, there is greater tendency to approach a donor close to the couple than there would be in the case of semen donation (where one can turn to a commercial bank). Given the negative societal judgment that seems to still evolve on adultery and incest, it is important that the issues be addressed directly in the preliminary counseling session.

Secrecy and Anonymity

The Ethics Committee recommends that physicians keep a record of sperm donations that maintains anonymity. Anonymous oocyte donation is technically more difficult to maintain, although protocols towards that end are being developed.[28] This anonymity is problematic to halakhists. There is the technical problem of fear of possible future incest. But this aside, there is a general concern within halakhah regarding an individual's pedigree, as "the *Shekhina* (Divine Presence) does not rest on an individual of unknown pedigree." Moreover, the anonymous quality trivializes the genetic components of character. Without minimizing the significance of the family environment or releasing any person from his or her individual responsibility for character development, rabbinic thought is of the opinion that character and psychological dispositions is to some extent inheritable. Anonymous donation makes light of this concern.

Conclusion

Halakhic Judaism shares all the moral concerns regarding heterologous artificial fertilization recorded in the dissent to the report of the Ethics Committee of the American Fertility Society. Yet, if technical halakhic objections can be overcome, halakha is willing to consider, on a case-by-case basis and in consultation with a rabbinic authority, heterologous artificial fertilization to the extent that it is a therapeutic technique for a distraught woman (or couple) who cannot be reconciled to either a childless marriage or adoption.

NOTES

1. Congregation for the doctrine of the Faith. "Instruction on Respect for Human Life in its Origin and on the Dignity of Procreation: Replies to Certain Questions of the Day." Reprinted in *Crux*, March 30, 1987.
2. Rabbi J.D. Bleich, "Abortion in Halakhic Literature." Tradition 10:2, 1968. Reprinted in J.D. Bleich, *Contemporary Halakhic Problems*, New York, 1977.
3. Rabbi Y. Zilberstein, "Fetal Reduction," *Assia*, nos. 45-46 (12:1-2), 1989.
4. A.S. Avraham, *Nishmat Avraham: Even HaEzer/Hoshem Mishpat* p. 234, Jerusalem, 5747, (1987).
5. Rabbi H.D. Halevi, "On Fetal Reduction," *Assia*, nos. 47-48 (12:3-4), 1990.
6. Rabbi M. Eliyahu, "Discarding Fertilized Eggs and Fetal Reduction," *Tehumin*, vol. 11, 1991.
7. Rabbi J.D. Bleich, "Fetal Tissue Research: Jewish Tradition and Public Policy," Tradition 24:4, 1989.
8. A.H. Handyside, J.K. Pattinson, R.J. Penketh, J.D. Frlhsnyu, R.M.L. Winston, E.G.D. Tuddenham, "Biopsy of human preimplantation embryos and sexing by DNA amplification," Lancet 347, 1989.
9. Rabbi J.D. Bleich, *Judaism and Healing: Halakhic Perspectives*, New York, Ktav, 1981, p. 111.
10. P.W. Zarutskie, et al, "The Clinical Relevance of Sex Selection Techniques," Fertil Steril 52(6):903, 1989.
11. Rabbi Y.B. Shafran, Opinion, Department of Halakha and Medicine of the Jerusalem Religious Council, 15 Shevat 5751 [30 January 1991].
12. Rabbi Y. Zilberstein, Responsum to Richard Grazi, Shevat 5751 [February 1991].
13. Rabbi J.B. Soloveitchick, "The Lonely Man of Faith," Tradition 7:2, 1965, p. 16.

14. J.E. Buster, "Embryo Donation by Uterine Flushing and Embryo Transfer," Clin Obstet Gynecol 12:4, 1985.
15. M.V. Sauer, R.E. Anderson, R.J. Paulson, "A Trial of Superovulation in Ovum Donors Undergoing Uterine Lavage," Fertil Steril 51(1):131, 1989.
16. Rabbi Y.B. Shafran, Communication to Joel B. Wolowelsky, April 1, 1991.
17. Rabbi J. Teitelbaum, "Responsum on Donor Artificial Insemination," *HaMa-or* 15(9):3-13, 1954.
18. Rabbi M. Feinstein, "Responsum to Mordecai Yaakov Berish" (5725 [1955]). Published in M.Y. Berish, *Helkat Yaakov* (Benai Brak, 5735 [1965]), volume 3, sections 47-52. Rabbi M. Feinstein, Responsa Iggerot Moshe. Part One (Brooklyn, NY: Moriah, 1961), responsum 71, pp. 169-171. Part Two (Brooklyn, NY: Moriah, 1963), responsum 11, pp. 322-324. Part Three (Brooklyn, NY: Moriah, 1973), responsum 14, pp. 436f. Part Four (Brooklyn, NY: Moria, 1985), responsum 32 (5), pp 75f.
19. S.C. Klock, D. Maier, "Psychological Factors Related to Donor Insemination," Fertil Steril, 56(3):489, 1991.
20. Rabbi E.Y. Waldenberg, Responsa Tsits Eliezer (Jerusalem: 5745 (1985)], vol. 9, no. 51, section 4, pp. 240-259.
21. Rabbi Y.Y. Weis, Responsa Minhat Yitzhak (London, 5727 [1957]), vol. 4, responsum 6.
22. Rabbi A. Lichtenstein, "Abortion: A Halakhic Perspective," Tradition 25(4):11, 1991.
23. Rabbi Sh. Z. Auerbach, "Hazra-a Melakhutit," *Noam*, Vol. 1 (Jerusalem: Mosad Harav Kook, 5718 [1958]), p. 166.
24. Rabbi J.D. Bleich, "In Vitro Fertilization: Questions of Maternal Identity and Cnversion," Tradition 25(4): 82-

102, 1991.
25. J.A. Robertson, "Ethical and Legal Issues in Human Egg Donation," Fertil Steril 52(3):353, 1989.
26. M.V. Sauer, et al, "Survey of Attitudes Regarding the Use of Siblings for Gamete Donation," Fertil Steril 49(4):721-722, 1988.
27. Rabbi Y.B. Shafran, Opinion, Office of Halakha and Medicine of the Jerusalem Chief Rabbinate. April 1, 1991.
28. R. Frydman, H. Letur-Konirsch, D de Ziegler, M. Bydlowski, A. Raoul-Duval, J. Selva, "A Protocol for Satisfying Ethical Issues Raised by Oocyte Donation: The Free, Anonymous, and Fertile Donors," Fertil Steril 53(4):666, 1990.

V. Afterword

AFTERWORD

"Everything that can be invented has been invented," asserted Charles Duell, the commissioner of patents, in 1899. Millions of patents later, such naivete is no longer possible. Indeed, despite the technological advances we have seen in all aspects of life, most of us understand that we are only at the beginning of a new era. This is no less true in medicine. While we have made dramatic inroads in our understanding and treatment of many diseases, it is likely that most of what will be clinically useful to doctors a hundred years hence is yet to be discovered.

It is impossible, under the circumstances, to have even attempted a definitive work on our subject. Shortly before this book went to press, for example, the procedure for cloning embryos was described. Tomorrow will always bring an additional technique, just as surely as it will see an additional controversy. What should be obvious to those who have digested the foregoing, however, is that the halakhic process is ever a participant in the ongoing discussion.

It is a precept amongst those who commit themselves to live within the guidelines of the halakha that the process by which this legal system has developed is a living one. *V'hai bahem*, the Creator says about His commandments. These are My laws, that you should live by them. As long as there are issues in this life to deal with, the halakhic process will be responsive to them. Indeed, we have witnessed that this is true in all areas of medicine, where complex issues have been confronted and discussed by many contemporary halakhic authorities. The sometimes divergent conclusions that they have reached is reflective of the dynamic exchange of viewpoints that is at the core of the living halakha and which has spawned such diversity within the Orthodox Jewish community.

This text, then, is a first in several respects. It is the first that focused exclusively on halakhic discussions that bear on the evaluation and treatment of infertility. In all likelihood, it will not be the last. Perhaps more importantly, it has brought together information from the discrete areas of halakha and medicine in a way that highlights their areas of overlap. After reading through the preceding chapters, those who stand on either side of the divide need not feel estranged by the other. The halakha anticipates and respects advances in medical science, and the practice of advanced medicine lends itself to the guidelines of the halakha. Couples who are coping with infertility must not feel obliged to choose between one and the other. Rather, they should find the two complementary.

Finally, this work has called on an audience which is unusual in its makeup. Unlike many other halakhic/medical issues, which tend to emerge on the practical level unexpectedly and for limited periods of time, the halakhic demands on fertility therapy pose a recurring challenge to infertile couples, their doctors and their rabbis. We therefore directed our essays simultaneously to all three groups. Where we have fallen short in this daunting task, we ask patience. This is just the beginning of the discussion. It will develop further, no doubt, as time goes by. In the interim, we hope this work has informed and encouraged Jewish couples undergoing fertility therapy.

AN EXPLANATION OF RABBINIC TERMS USED IN THIS BOOK

Halakha is the legal and ethical system of rabbinic Judaism. Biblical law generally refers to rulings found in the Pentateuch (the first five books of the Hebrew Bible). It also includes rulings not explicitly mentioned in the Bible but which are viewed as Biblical by the rabbis. Generally, rabbinic authorities have very little leeway in modifying Biblical laws.

Rabbinic law refers to requirements and restrictions imposed by the early rabbinic authorities and codified in the Mishnah and Talmud, which, together with the Bible, form the primary texts of rabbinic Judaism. Rabbinic authorities have some extra leeway in modifying rabbinic laws, but cannot amend them at will or dismiss them.

The basic sources for the investigation of halakhic positions on any ethical or legal issue are the Bible, the Mishnah and Talmud, and universally accepted codifications such as Maimonides' medieval *Mishne Torah* or Karo's later *Shulhan Arukh*. But rulings on contemporary issues cannot be promulgated by any central authority, as there is no formal hierarchal structure to the various rabbinic authorities and courts currently functioning. Positions on contemporary issues are developed by circulation of responsa (rabbinic rulings) to questions posed to various rabbinic authorities.

These responsa are issued individually and eventually are published in a volume or series of volumes, sometimes posthumously. Collegial review and community acceptance eventually allow for specific opinions to emerge as dominant. Yet, even when one view surfaces as authoritative, individual rabbis or layman will often defer to their local authority, whose position is considered decisive.

P'ru ur'vu is the Hebrew phrase for "be fruitful and multiply," the commandment/blessing contained in the first chapter of Genesis.

Niddah is the state induced by the onset of a woman's menstrual period and which continues until she immerses herself at the specified time in a natural body of water or a specially constructed pool called a *mikveh*. Biblical and rabbinic law prohibit a woman who is in a state of *niddah* from having any physical contact (including but not limited to intercourse) with her husband.

Generally, any type of uterine blood flow induces a state of *niddah*, even if it is not a result of the woman's normal menstrual flow, while an artificially induced wound (a *makkah*) does not. The consequences of these halakhic categories are discussed in detail in this book. While the concept is foreign to most non-observant people, it is a core value in halakhic Judaism which has great impact on an observant couple's married life.

Halakhic Sabbath and holiday laws include a number of prohibited activities; *muktzeh* refers to those objects which cannot be handled because of their association with these prohibited activities.

CONTRIBUTORS

Sara L.F. Barris, Psy.D.
Clinical Psychologist
Director of Support Groups
RESOLVE, NYC

Rabbi Hershel Billet
Rabbi, Young Israel of Woodmere
Lecturer and Director of Publications
Genesis Foundation

Joel J.K. Comet, Ph.D.
Clinical Psychologist
Leader of Support Groups
RESOLVE, NYC

Richard V. Grazi, M.D.
Director Division of Reproductive
        Endocrinology and Infertility
Maimonides Medical Center
Assistant Professor, Obstetrics and Gynecology
SUNY Health Science Center ad Brooklyn

Julian Yoel Jakobovits, M.D.
Instructor in Medicine
Department of Medicine
Division of General Medicine
Division of Gastroenterology
The Johns Hopkins University School of Medicine

Rabbi Allen Schwartz
Instructor of Bible
Yeshiva University
Senior Rabbi
Congregation Ohab Zedek, New York

Rabbi Richard B. Weiss, M.D.
Department of Medicine
Maimonides Medical Center
Brooklyn, New York

Joel B. Wolowelsky, Ph.D.
Chairman, Advanced Placement Studies
Yeshivah of Flatbush
Brooklyn, New York
Associate Editor, *Tradition*